THE TRUST MANIFESTO

THE TRUST MANIFESTO

What You Need to Do to
Create a Better Internet

Damian Bradfield

BUSINESS

PENGUIN BUSINESS

UK | USA | Canada | Ireland | Australia
India | New Zealand | South Africa

Penguin Business is part of the Penguin Random House group of companies
whose addresses can be found at global.penguinrandomhouse.com.

First published 2019
001

With thanks to Calcanet Press for permission to use 'Ode to Bill' by John Ashbery on page 12,
taken from *John Ashbery: Collected Poems 1956–1987* © Calcanet Press UK, 2010; Rough Trade
Publishing for the David Berman lyrics on page 29 © David Berman, 2008; and Trevor Paglen for the
photograph on page 68 © Trevor Paglen, 2015.

Set in 12/17.25 pt Optima LT Std
Typeset by Jouve (UK), Milton Keynes
Printed and bound in Great Britain by Clays Ltd, Elcograf S.p.A.

A CIP catalogue record for this book is available from the British Library

ISBN: 978–0–241–36984–5

www.greenpenguin.co.uk

MIX
Paper from
responsible sources
FSC® C018179

Penguin Random House is committed to a
sustainable future for our business, our readers
and our planet. This book is made from Forest
Stewardship Council® certified paper.

Contents

CONTENTS

Prologue

You need to buy shoes.

Your running shoes are falling apart.

It's only a matter of time before a sole starts flapping.

As you wander closer to the displays at the shoe shop, you're approached by one of the employees.

You've been dealing with sales pitches for as long as you've been shopping, which is almost as long as you've been alive.

You're used to both the soft and hard sell, the obsequious attention and the dealings of a hassled employee.

This employee is unobtrusive.

Even now it would be difficult to describe him.

He's just a guy, an extension of the store, a helping hand who would like to make a sale.

As you're talking to him you have a thought.

You know what?

There's that other shoe store.

It's further away, but it's worth a shot.

They stock sensible shoes.

Sensible running shoes might be a good thing these days.

So, after looking at a couple of pairs, and even trying on some Nikes, and walking a few feet in them, feeling for pinching in the toes, you turn to the sales associate and tell him what you've told people working in stores for all your shopping life: 'I really appreciate the help.'

Then you're out of there, and the door closes.

You walk to the corner and wait to cross the road.

You've got other stuff on your mind, so you don't immediately recognize the person standing beside you, looking at you.

Where have you seen that sandy-blond hair before?

Where have you seen that face?

It's the sales associate.

That's weird.

He must move with speed.

Perhaps it's one of the reasons why he got a job at a store selling athletic shoes.

After you give him a weak smile, a smile you hope will act as a farewell, he says, 'Are you sure you don't want those Nikes?'

'The Nikes I tried on?' you ask.

'Yes,' he responds. 'I've got a photo of them right here.'

So you give it a cursory glance and then say, again, 'Thank you, no.'

You walk away, and you don't look back to see if the guy is following you because you don't want to encourage him in any way.

One way of taking your mind off that odd experience is to buy vegetables for dinner. There's a supermarket nearby, a calming place, especially the vegetable section, especially when the overhead sprays come on to dampen all the produce.

You're looking at the apples.

Then you notice something, or someone, a man hiding behind the pyramid of apples.

When you edge closer you notice it's the guy from the shoe store.

He's crouched down, staring up at you with – you've got to admit it – a fervent look in his eyes.

'Hi, I'm just wondering if you've reconsidered,' he says in that insistent voice.

'Reconsidered what?' you ask.

You check to see if there's a grocery store employee nearby, just in case.

'Reconsidered the shoes,' he says. 'I've got a photo of them here.'

And he rises out of his squat to show you the photo.

'I really don't need to see that photo,' you say.

'They come in other colours,' he replies, 'and it's a great deal.'

'Look,' you reply, 'I left your store.

'I'm not interested, and even if I was, I don't appreciate you popping up like this while I'm in another store.

'Is it even legal for you to be behaving like this?'

He doesn't say anything.

He stands very still.

Now things get strange.

As you're walking home you can see him in other stores, staring out of the windows as you pass by.

And when you arrive home and set the groceries down to grab the mail, you open the mailbox to find it's already packed with flyers and mailouts and newsletters from the shoe store, and there's that photo of the same pair of Nikes.

It's dark but you begin to sense something, a presence, in the darkness.

And sure enough, when you turn on the light, there's the sales associate, with his bland face, and that look in his eyes, sitting on your couch like there's nothing wrong, like it's fine to be in your space, to know your habits, to follow you around – that blankness is not the look of someone engaging in behaviour they know to be bad, or even questionable.

He's just looking at you.

'You'd be surprised,' he says, 'how much I know about you.

'I'd be happy to suggest some other shoes you might like based on your trip to the store.'

'I wouldn't like that, thank you,' you say, somehow still dealing with this guy with a politeness he seems to have forgotten.

In days gone past this would have been called home intrusion.

'Would you like me to show you the shoes again?' he asks.

Is there something wrong here?

Is there a reason why he doesn't seem fazed by this?

Are you the problem in that you remember, somewhere in the recesses of your mind, a world before both our shopping habits and our sense of privacy got capsized?

'People don't mind this,' the man says, and you think of how often a statement like this has been used to justify change.

You're guilty of it.

'People live their life on smartphones,' you yourself announced a while ago.

You don't want a scene.

You did, after all, go into the store.

But when you ask him to leave he looks at you, again, with that look of a man who has done nothing wrong, who is unimpeachably innocent, and says, 'That's fine.

'But could you fill out this survey first?'

*

This book is for people whose professional and personal lives have been upended by technology.

It's for those who are now required to be 'always on', for

those who have been drawn into lives of convenience at all cost.

It's for those who want to read short sentences and then get angry.

It's for those who want to question the online status quo and explore the possibilities of the internet, perhaps even envision a future where we finally understand the effects of spam, clickbait and attention-sapping media.

I'm not Jaron Lanier, or any other tech seer you'd like to name.

I'm not a genius.

I can talk from a position of a touch of success.

This is all based on real-life experiences within a (soon to be) billion-dollar company, WeTransfer.

The book will view the world from both inside and outside the bubble.

It will include the voices of those operating within tech and those on the fringe.

Most importantly, I'd like – in some small way – to encourage people to consider who they trust, how they should pay for the internet, and whether they are prepared to keep providing their own data, the totality of their online lives, to private companies – like an endless font, like an endlessly spouting oil well.

After all, what is the cost?

PART ONE
Scoping the Problem

1: The Recap

Let's survey the landscape, shall we?

Let's examine where we're at with fresh eyes.

And ears.

'Every move you make on the Internet is worth some tiny amount to someone,' journalist Alexis Madrigal once wrote in *The Atlantic*, 'and a panoply of companies want to make sure that no step along your Internet journey goes unmonetized.'

That saddened me.

And made me a little angry.

No step, no tiptoe will be taken for free.

When the article was written, way back in 2012, a lifetime ago in our digital age, Madrigal found that 105 companies tracked his movements over a 36-hour period.

That's just the start.

So let's reflect.

You begin your day.

You turn on your phone.

You open your computer.

Immediately your browser starts yielding data.

Immediately you offer up a unique fingerprint to the web: 'your very own specific mix of browser software, hardware, default language, even the fonts you have installed – which can identify you even without any other information.'

That's how David Nield, a reporter from *Gizmodo*, described it.

'Roam the web for five minutes,' John Cheney-Lippold writes in his book *We Are Data: Algorithms and the Making of Our Digital Selves*. 'In a period of time only slightly longer than the average television commercial break, you will have generated, through your web activity, an identity that is likely separate from the person who you thought you were.'

Like an ambitious baker, you start gathering cookies.

You continue building your daily browser history, which internet service providers can now sell to advertisers.

You're already leaking data.

You've already become a producer.

You're offering up a resource for free.

But don't spend all your time on the laptop.

Step away from the screen and interact with the new guest in our homes.

There's now a human voice emanating from a device on the counter telling you jokes and sports scores.

Did you think, when you were young, that one day you'd have a place in your home for a recording device?

About the only thing Amazon's Alexa can't do – yet – is answer the door.

But like a real child, Alexa's changing, growing, learning.

She shows great drive.

She's ambitious and goal-oriented.

She's interested in business, mostly retail.

In March 2018, the *New York Times* reported on a set of patent applications Amazon filed, in which: 'Amazon describes how a "voice sniffer algorithm" could be used on an array of devices.'

It would 'analyze audio almost in real time when it hears words like "love", "bought" or "dislike"'.

And then there was a diagram in the application 'which illustrated how a phone call between two friends could result in one receiving an offer for the San Diego Zoo and the other seeing an ad for a Wine of the Month Club membership'.

Good listening skills, Alexa.

There's no real point in keeping the communication overt.

'The Alexa Hunches function,' Karen Weise wrote in another *New York Times* article in September 2018, '. . . tries to provide suggestions; for instance, if a user says good night to Alexa, the voice assistant might note that a porch light is on and offer to turn it off.' The feature became available in late 2018.

'Good night,' she says. 'By the way, your living room light is on. Do you want me to turn it off?'

And if you want to answer her with a quieter voice, Alexa will now go *sotto voce*. 'Whisper Mode is a new feature that allows you to whisper to Alexa,' reported *Business Wire* in September, 2018, 'and she will whisper her response back to you.'

So nice of her to keep it down.

But doors? She's getting there.

For the entrance to your house we've already got Ring, the doorbell company Amazon acquired in 2018, which records every movement outside your front door.

Every face that appears at your doorstep is registered.

Connect Ring to ADT cameras you've got in your home, and every movement, inside and out, is recorded.

These tools are for your own security, online and off.

They're not scary.

Each element listed above represents just one thread in a modern life.

But in the world we live in, these threads are woven together.

Data combines with data combines with data to form patterns we couldn't conceive of years earlier.

The resulting tapestry is astoundingly complex.

We're living, after all, in high-thread-count times.

Now step outside the home.

Google Maps and Waze and Citymapper do their job and take you where you need to be (and collect that data).

The Fitbit on your wrist collects data on your movement,

heart rate and weight. Your phone and your laptop aren't resting either.

They gobble up IP addresses as you move and connect.

The list gets longer as you make your way through the world, building a scrapbook of digits.

If you stop to use Google Docs, your changes are saved.

But then so is the time of day.

Those numbers become indicators of when you've finally shaken your procrastination and become productive.

What is taking shape as these threads are woven together is not just an understanding of what you are – a productive person with a Fitbit on your wrist – but who you are.

Not who you think you are.

Not the rose-tinted version.

But rather, a more coherent view of yourself.

A more reliable biography is now produced outside yourself.

And it's incontrovertible.

The other day I visited the gym and when they asked me about my health I told them a story I thought was true.

I eat a healthy breakfast most mornings.

But that changed under interrogation.

It could have been mostly true.

The data said otherwise.

Now, more and more, we've got evidence that runs against the stories we tell ourselves.

These days, constructing your own narrative is a luxury.

The ability to compose an autobiography without giving in to data is disappearing.

In 2010, Eric Schmidt, at the time Chief Executive of Google said: 'There were 5 exabytes of information created between the dawn of civilization through 2003, but that much information is now created every 2 days.'

(The figure has now been amended to 7 days.)

If you're in your twenties or older, the story of your life was, for a long time, up for grabs. Those unmarked years were made up of days and days of masses of uncollected data.

Trips went unmarked.

Runs through the park were unaccounted for.

Experiences evaporated.

Advertisers made guesses.

*

But there's more to look at in the new digital landscape unfurling around us.

That thing out in the driveway, or tucked away in a garage?

It superficially looks like what we used to call a car.

But these days, when you look closer, it starts to resemble a data collection tool on wheels.

It's not just about where you go and how fast you get there, but how much you weigh, the speed of the car, your braking habits.

You may say you're not distracted. But General Motors' 2018 Cadillac CT6 with super cruise has an internal camera mounted on the steering column to monitor where drivers are looking, 'ensuring that they're watching the road ahead' wrote Patrick Olsen in *Consumer Reports* in June, 2018.

So: 'Data is the new oil for the car industry,' announced Apurva Kumar, a member of Forbes Technology Council.

There's a company called Otonomo that sucks up and analyses car data.

Like any ambitious company, they gather their wares and attempt to make a sale.

They endeavour to seek out third-party buyers to sell to, such as the obvious, like automakers.

But they're also reaching out to parking app developers or maybe even, according to an article by Peter Holley in the *Washington Post* in January, 2018, a company looking to plan out its billboard locations.

Their aim is to help.

Sorry – their aim is to help . . . automakers commercialize their data.

Car makers know the information coming from their vehicles will provide a rich section of the tapestry.

Here are the actual habits of people, actual destinations, actual routines.

The car will predict which shops you likely visited, which neighbourhoods you frequented.

You might be able to use the line: I walked to the gym a few times.

But it'll get more obvious the data says no.

*

The information used to stay in the car, but now it spurts forth like a geyser.

Cars are connected.

Holley reports that: 'a copy of an owner's manual for a Honda Clarity . . . notes that the vehicle is equipped with multiple monitoring systems that transmit data at a rate determined by Honda.'

Chetan Sharma Consulting revealed, as reported in an *Axios* story in February, 2018, that 2017 saw more new cars added to cellular networks than new cell phones.

AT&T has been adding a million or more new cars to its network each quarter for the last eleven quarters.

Verizon is set to make at least $1 billion from IoT (the internet of things) and telematics.

Smartphone penetration is at 84 per cent in the United States, and new customer revenue is approaching zero.

But connected cars are still new to the market, so as they roll off assembly lines and into garages, they'll need to be hooked up to a network.

It was a natural progression.

Previous research has suggested that, very soon, 98 per cent of new cars will be equipped with embedded modems.

The CEO of Otonomo, Ben Volkow, estimated that by 2020, bundling and selling data from connected cars will be a massive new revenue stream for the OEMs, in the order of billions of dollars a year.

*

Now park that car – sorry, I mean your mobile data collection centre – quickly.

It'll notice how close you are to the kerb.

And when you park that car and enter a building, you'll be on CCTV. The BBC once reported (in 2011): 'Britons are caught on camera 70 times a day on average, rather than up to 300 times as previously stated.' So it's not as bad as you thought. The relief!

And anyway, those CCTV cameras are looking so quaint these days.

I am not a technophobe.

I work in tech.

I am not knee-jerking against this.

This isn't a terrified scream.

Part of me thinks it would be great if Alexa turned off the porch lights for me.

But I am inviting an appraisal.

And why not?

Why the need for explanation?

What's wrong with collecting this data?

It's just sitting there.

Years ago, those who weren't on Facebook were told not to be elitist.

Don't appraise.

Just do it.

Use the service.

Why are you standing in the way?

How did we all quickly become defensive?

And now, years later, how do we learn to appraise this life we're living?

Isn't it okay to visit our collective past and, instead of mourning, remember the purpose of how we used to live?

Those unmarked years served a purpose . . .

Our movements, our paths, our routines used to disappear.

We used to live our lives letting go of experience, watching it pass into the past.

Experience became malleable.

There were no numbers to back it up, forever etched somewhere.

These days, I'm reminded of a few lines from the John Ashbery poem called 'Ode to Bill'.

On the great, relaxed curve of time,

All the forgotten springs, dropped pebbles,

Songs once heard that then passed out of light

Into everyday oblivion?

Songs once heard passing out of the light are increasingly rare these days.
There is no such thing as everyday oblivion.

Was everyday oblivion only there because we hadn't yet invented ways to track ourselves? I tend to think it served a more important purpose.

The right to be forgotten was not a political term. It was a universal dictate.

When a detective asks a character in David Lynch's *Lost Highway* whether or not he owns a video camera, the man responds: 'I like to remember things my own way . . . not necessarily how they happened.'

So back to our day.

Our finances have been monitored, our movements, and now we move on to our thoughts.

I think about Ashbery's words when I view how my kids are growing up.

There are not many things that haven't been put on to a phone.

Everything my son is doing at school – every piece of content that he's writing, every project he's working on – is online.

Everything.

He doesn't write anything in a book.

Or if he does, it will be copied and put into a Google Doc, to submit to the teacher, to then approve.

That's his written project work.

Every presentation they're working on as a team is on Google Docs.

His grammar is corrected by a program called Alexis.

Reading Plus is a program to help him speed-read.

Everything that he's read is being tracked on a system.

Every update, every school appraisal, every fundraising event is sent to my Gmail.

Pretty much his entire existence at school is being sent through a Google company at a certain point.

Maybe, in the terms and conditions, it says the companies he and his school interact with will never sell the data.

But if one of these smaller companies is sold, does that promise still apply?

That long thread of information, combined with social media and every piece of technology he lets into his life, is going to grow into what could be mildly described as a profile.

It will, over time, reveal the kind of acute character description that used to more commonly exist in the realm of Russian novelists.

The depths of people, the vastness of this data, the myriad threads.

What kind of banker or lawyer would ever need to turn to novels if they spent their day poring over this tapestry?

And judging, of course.

This objective, complete view of a human is constructed, obviously, for commercial uses.

That's been clear from the beginning.

But even a previous phase of this relationship is starting to fade into history.

The phrase 'you are the product' might have someday, back in the past, carried a weighty significance.

But it also implied a finite act.

I'm being used.

But at some point, the purpose will be done.

I will have been used.

'If you're not paying for it,' they used to say, 'you're the product.'

How twee.

The more I think about it, the more I feel that I'm not a product – used once or twice, or even many times – but now, like my children, like you, I'm a process, a lifelong provider, an oil well.

And because the process has been slow, and because I have been too lazy to pore over terms and conditions and consider alternatives, and certainly unable to consider that what came before might have had merit, I've begun to resemble less of a human being and more of a large underground reserve.

I may not know it, or may refuse to pay attention to it, but I'm going to get fracked for the rest of my life.

This is an arrangement that will continue to benefit the data collectors.

It'll continue until we do something different.

It's new.

We're getting manipulated, but we haven't quite figured out what to do to end – or even minimize – the manipulation.

And what of the other side?

Full disclosure: that's where I sit during the working day.

My company gathers data.

We've made a lot of money from advertising.

I am not living off-grid.

But I'm troubled by what I see around me from the men and women in the industry.

I know we have to move forward, but at what cost?

We can gather data, but what is the quality of that data going to be?

We have ways of dredging it, scraping it, stealing it, grasping it.

We have perfected geotracking techniques.

We have recorded people without them knowing.

We've lost sight of what it is we're really doing.

Some days, I look around and think we've become acceptable stalkers, crouched in someone's darkened apartment, waiting for them to come home, with a photo of a pair of Nikes on the screen of our phone. *This is okay.*

There's the pestering.

There's the mining for data.

And, increasingly, there are the moments when the threads are woven together.

Trust us, the companies and entities around us say.

Trust us to keep you and your data safe.

For people looking for a romantic partner, they trust that they'll be able to use dating apps to present a version of themselves that will entice others.

It's just that now social scoring is being combined with credit scoring in an attempt to judge and assess partnerships.

Swipe right if they've got good credit.

Dating apps might be scary.

This enters even scarier territory.

We don't need Jane Austen to tell you the importance of financial security in matchmaking.

Bloomberg reported that a 2017 survey from the parent company of Tinder found that financial responsibility was ranked as a very or extremely important quality in a potential mate by 69 per cent of 2,000 online daters surveyed.

'That placed it ahead of sense of humor (67 percent), attractiveness (51 percent), ambition (50 percent), courage (42 percent), and modesty (39 percent),' wrote Suzanne Woolley.

'A good credit score was associated with being responsible, trustworthy, and smart.'

A person's Tinder profile and credit score are two strands that are increasingly easy to weave together.

In many cultures, financial stability and well-being are incredibly important factors in selecting a romantic partner.

If you can assess somebody based on not only their looks and their intelligence but also their credit score, you're securing yourself a perfect life partner.

Or so the thinking goes.

The infamous example came when Baihe, China's biggest matchmaking service, teamed up with the financial wing of the online shopping platform Alibaba, to showcase clients with beautiful, well-toned credit scores, giving them pride of place on the site.

Again, the narrative of our lives is being wrested away from us.

Some sort of story arises from the alchemy of bringing these two strands together.

We'd better trust tech to tell a beneficial story.

Because who's going to choose someone with a crap credit score?

Or someone who's in the process of changing their life?

The numbers don't track ethereal qualities, such as potential.

No one is allowed growth or mistakes.

What are people going to do?

What if you're in a state where you've done something wrong?

You went on holiday, and your automated direct deposit didn't work on two occasions.

Your credit score plummets.

You've had a bad run with boyfriends, and you haven't met anybody for the last six months. How are you going to keep things in check?

You're already low.

There is no numeric system for empathy that can be placed alongside these strands.

The system is now saying, 'You're not suitable, we've got nobody for you.'

You're out of work.

You don't have a girlfriend.

Your rental agreement's up for renewal.

Somebody is going to default to a credit scoring company to look at what you've been up to. They're not going to employ empathy.

Without empathy, without a human interacting and discussing something with you, odds are they won't make a decision that's going to be beneficial for you.

For many of us manga was alien at the beginning.

Look what happened.

Get ready for the manga of relationships and dating.

Get ready as the ideas of eastern social credit are adopted by the west.

VCs and big business will notice how much money it generates.

They'll be keen.

I can't imagine credit scoring companies will complain.

Credit scoring companies are eager to expand.

Even after their own data breach controversy, Equifax is growing bigger.

Equifax was a company that started close to where I used to live, in Canterbury, in the UK.

Back then, when I was a kid, Equifax was a mystery to me.

They had huge headquarters.

No one really knew too much about what they were doing.

Credit scoring was quite primitive in the 1980s, compared with today.

Every financial institution, loan company, mortgage provider, savings institution, is reliant on that information.

Why not spread further?

Equifax has weathered its own battering.

It's evident we can't always trust credit scoring companies.

But here we are.

And what if we look at credit scoring through the prism of diversity and equal rights?

If this data becomes increasingly important for some sort of existence, we're alienating the less fortunate.

You use a prepaid credit card.

You're renting a house.

You don't have good credit so you're renting it in your girl-friend's name.

You're basically non-existent.

You don't exist.

How do you claw yourself out of that situation?

Who's going to give you the break to get you on the ladder?

In order to play, in order to date, in order to live, in order to be in society, we must give up data.

In the process, data becomes a great normalizing tool.

It's a funnelling process.

You might be able to remain outside of it in some ways, but there is pressure to take part.

There's an inherent trust that it's all good.

Don't drag your feet.

Sign the terms and conditions.

What happens if you don't sign the terms and conditions?

What happens if you don't opt in? You're opting out, which means most of the time you don't get the service that's being offered.

Will there come a time when companies will pay honestly for the raw material of data, as a sculptor would pay for her clay?

I feel this issue from both sides, and I know I'm not the only one working in an industry that depends on data collection but at the same time thinking: Is this how it's supposed to be?

My favourite question for data scientists is: What did you want to achieve when you started?

When you were a kid, did you dream you'd be able to learn so much about a person that you'd be able to market to them on a granular, almost cellular, level?

Did you think you'd join a cult called data?

Did you dream of capturing every heartbeat from the people around you?

Did you dream of becoming a socially acceptable stalker?

I don't use the term lightly.

Here we are.

Following people.

Tracking people.

I don't know many people who, at the beginning, heard of the possibilities of the internet and hoped we'd have data scraping instead of Tim Berners-Lee's vision.

What child grows up hoping to data scrape?

*

Something's happening, even on my side of things.

There are a lot of metaphors for data and, unsurprisingly, the clichés abound.

Collecting data streams is the best thing since sliced bread, I've been told by bright-faced techies with a love for dead metaphor.

But we need to look at this profusion, this surplus.

We need to look at what we're doing to get it.

We need to examine the bonds of trust in this industry.

Data may be the best thing since sliced bread.

But it's white bread.

And we're eating and eating, ripping open those plastic bags like there's no consequence.

Like it's good for us.

*

This book isn't going to solve the problem.

All I can hope to do is nudge a few people.

These days, in the conversations about the direction of the tech industry, there are more and more ex-tech people discussing why they left Facebook, or how sorry they are for inventing the banner ad, or the pop-up.

This group of people made their money and now want to apologize.

Great.

At least they stopped.

But what if they had started the conversation from within?

What if they had started these conversations without leaving the table?

What if they'd tried to make a change or a difference from within their organization?

My company, WeTransfer, is an ad-funded business.
We need data to sell advertising.
We aren't a non-profit.
We aren't a foundation.
WeTransfer has to make money.
We need to monetize our site.
But there's got to be a different way.
We want to do so in a way that is ethical and as frictionless as possible.
And we want to continue to discuss both what works and what should work.
A company should be able to press forward and at the same time examine and plot out paths for change.

People out there are looking for help.
They're looking for guidance.
They want suggestions on who to trust and listen to, and which sources are reliable.
The rise of populism in the US and Europe has exacerbated the situation.
The erosion of public trust in political leaders has been coupled with the movement to end net neutrality.
Again and again, journalists, policy makers and concerned citizens have called for greater regulation.
This group of people – myself included – want decisions to

be made on the laws that currently allow monopolies to flourish on the web.

Now is the time.

The topic of trust appears in editorials, in discussions, from tech sector blogs to the *New York Times*.

Every day the erosion of trust continues.

It's happening in politics, in everyday life and online.

It's happening in the corporate world with Uber, Facebook, Google, Equifax – the list goes on.

We ask for trust.

But do we in the tech sector deserve it?

Once we've harvested data from our social media, shopping habits, even our own brain, where do we go with it?

Naturally, our answer always seems to be: forwards.

In this industry, we've got a real talent for pushing forward without safeguards.

When it comes to our health: In July, 2018, the NHS in the UK was found to have illegally handed 1.6 million patient records – including information such as HIV status and mental health history – to Google's artificial intelligence company DeepMind.

When it comes to our homes: In August, 2018, the US Department of Housing and Urban Development 'filed a discrimination complaint against Facebook for giving landlords and home sellers tools that let them prevent citizens with disabilities, people of some religious faiths and members of racial minority groups from seeing certain housing ads', reported Mason Marks in the *Washington Post*.

When it comes to our cars: We're told not to worry because in a 2014 letter to the Federal Trade Commission, 'automakers pledged to abide by a set of privacy policies that included not sharing information with third parties without owners' consent.'

But in the *Washington Post*, Ryan Calo, an associate professor of law at the University of Washington, who teaches courses on robotics law and policy, said, 'Ultimately, there's no car privacy statute that car companies have to abide by.'

Trust us.

Trust the data collectors.

'Not only are automakers collecting a lot of data, they don't have a particular regime that is regulating how they do it.'

The more data a company collects, the more incentive the company has to monetize that data.

2: When Do We Ask for a New Internet?

It's an honest question.

When do we appraise this thing that's been built?

Have you answered this question for yourself?

Have you taken the time?

And are your answers the same now as they've always been?

In 2010, would you have said: 'You know, we need to appraise this thing we call the internet as soon as it's used to polarize a populace and install a leader with authoritarian tendencies in the US?

'That's when we'll do it.

'No more fooling around.'

In 2012, would you have said: 'We need to take stock of this thing we've all built when the prospect of net neutrality is threatened.

'That's when we'll do it.

'Seriously.

'No more messing.'

Perhaps you realized we needed to appraise the situation when Edward Snowden appeared on the scene.

Perhaps it was when you realized some of the websites of your favourite small businesses could soon be loading at a slower rate because they can't pay for preferential treatment.

(Perhaps it'll be that moment when you're sitting looking at a screen waiting for that boutique's page to load and you're thinking: Is there something wrong with my connection? What was net neutrality, anyway?)

Maybe it was the moment you tried to pinpoint just when, during the day, you weren't interacting with Google in some way.

Maybe it was when you loaded up Facebook for the twenty-seventh time in a day and whispered to yourself: What am I *doing*?

Why am I *acting* this way?

Maybe it was that moment you looked at Mark Zuckerberg's face during congressional hearings watched by millions.

You thought: Why do I have to live in your world?

Out of all the people out there, why do I have to live in *your* world?

You thought: Could you do yourself a favour and blink once in a while?

Dude: blink! Your eyeballs are drying out.

At one point, maybe you read a news story about Cambridge Analytica.

You really tried to figure out what was going on with that scandal.

You took a break to check social media.

You took a break to pay a bill.

You took a break to answer an email.

You thought to yourself: Why can't I just read one news story all the way through?

Maybe you considered the possibility of an appraisal of the internet when you fully comprehended the Cambridge Analytica story.

Or maybe you thought: I'll give it one more scandal.

But that's all you're getting, internet.

One more major privacy scandal.

Maybe you ignored Equifax.

You've got stuff to do.

Or maybe it was the moment you were hacked.

Or the moment you thought: Have I been hacked?

Or the moment you caught yourself saying: 'I don't really care if I'm hacked.'

Or you heard someone say: 'If you're not doing anything wrong, why should you even be worried?'

When you consider Instagram, perhaps you thought to yourself: It *is* crazy.

Imagine going through adolescence assessing your self-worth every ten minutes.

Offering up all this free content, photo by photo.

Imagine the upkeep.

Imagine trying to negotiate this perilous, ever-shifting territory.

And doing it every day, on top of everything else.

Then you think of your own Instagram habits.

The jealousy.

The petty emotions that flare up.

You say they don't.

They do.

You're not a teenager.

Maybe you thought: We should take a look at what Instagram is doing to our society as soon as I start acting like one of those teenagers.

And while you were thinking this you liked a few photos.

What's your uncrossable line?

When do you say okay, wait a second?

Is it when a metaphor actually makes sense to you?

What we've created is a gilded cage?

What we've created is a candy jail?

Maybe it's when you heed the words of David Berman, the greatest unsung songwriter of our generation.

He wrote the song 'Candy Jail':

Life in a candy jail / With peppermint bars / Peanut brittle bunk beds / And marshmallow walls / Where the guards are gracious / And the grounds are grand / And the warden keeps the data on your favorite brands . . .

When is it?

When is enough enough?

When self-regulation has obviously failed?

When equality has disappeared from this realm too?

When the internet where you are is no longer the same internet as they've got in Ghana?

When Tim Berners-Lee, inventor of the worldwide web, shakes his head woefully?

When will you finally be ready for some sort of change?

Maybe never?

How's never for you?

3: The Age of Trust

We're living in an extraordinary age: the age of trust.

We believe the intricate system we've constructed will remain reliable and never falter.

We're confident enough to place much of our life online.

We expect the world to work for us.

Every day we expect feats to be accomplished that would have been impossible, even twenty years ago.

Our expectations are heightened.

When you step away to consider it, our lives are wondrous in what we take for granted.

We're in danger of becoming the sort of people who complain about the food on the flight without taking into account they're hurtling through the air.

We take the advancements for granted.

Everyone's parent has a new knee.

We trust software all day, every day.

We trust the language of algorithms.

We trust software to correct our most personal creative mistakes.

'You're recording a song and find a note that is really quite out of tune,' Brian Eno told *The Vinyl Factory* a few years ago.

'In the past, you'd have said, it's a great performance, so we'll just live with it.

'What you do now is retune that note.'

We trust we'll be able to make things better, even at a cost.

'So you're always asking yourself, have we lost something of the tension of the performance, of the feeling of humanity and vulnerability and organic truth or whatever, by making these corrections?'

Maybe so. But we trust that, overall, these developments are helpful.

From the moment the alarms on our phones sound in the morning to the moment we set them again at night, we trust in a varied and intricate web of interactions.

We slide money back and forth online, consult navigational systems, forego old technologies, such as keys, for the fobs in our pockets.

We touch screens all day without understanding touch-screen technology.

We lift the hoods of our cars and fail to recognize what's inside.

We trust that proprietary software will get us from A to B.

We're taught as children not to get into the cars of strangers.

Now, Uber in hand, we slide into strange cars every day and expectantly look at the driver in the front seat.

'Your name is Jason, right?'

*

These are shifting, counter-intuitive times.

Imagine telling your ten-year-old self: 'When you get older, everyone will voluntarily carry with them a tracking device at all times.

'For many, it'll be the first thing they look at in the morning and the last thing they consult at night.'

There is risk and wonder embedded within the banality of our normal working days.

But you can't be in awe of it 24/7.

You can't walk around permanently wide-eyed.

Who wants to live their life thanking the motherboard each time the computer surges to life?

Still: acknowledge that trust is more widespread than ever.

We've suddenly become very, very trusting beings.

It's happened in only a handful of years.

Would you like Google to remember this password for you?

Sure.

I trust it with everything else.

The friendly interface of technology obscures the magnitude of what is going on here.

If we take for granted the importance, and the strangeness, of these interactions, we risk losing a chance to comprehend what we've gained.

Wake up with your phone, glance at an Apple watch, employ Shazam to grab a song flitting past you in the coffee shop, trace your pathway with GPS, slide that CVS rewards card into the reader, pay with FasTrak or E-ZPass, use Nest to control the thermostat from your phone or computer.

It evokes a multi-part symphony of life.

Apple TV, Fire Stick, Roku, Kindle and NOOK.

WeTransfer is part of this new behaviour.

My company is part of this growing din.

I speak of this trust from the inside.

We're a part of the lives of billions of people.

Users send files.

But these are not simply strings of code or operational instructions.

These are memories, secrets, unpublished manuscripts, personal photos, business ideas.

Users entrust part of their life to us.

They might not understand how that file shows up in exactly the expected destination, but they trust that it will.

Not only do we trust new devices and services, we also trust the companies who own them.

We trust companies with our details, our data, our choices, our shopping records, our interactions in shoe stores and grocery stores, and everything in between, even our movements in space.

We've been dealing with them long enough to wonder what happens when the trust breaks down.

Because we're living our lives online, it's worth asking

the question: Is the internet heading in a more trustworthy direction?

Every day, new evidence emerges to say: Maybe not.

There's an onslaught.

In October 2018, as reported by *Business Insider*, news broke of 'a bug in the company's Google+ social network that affected an estimated 500,000 people and exposed information that users intended to keep private'.

That's just one particular week.

It seems to me that rather than saying companies are trustworthy or not, it's worth examining a new kind of trust that is being asked of us.

Increasingly, there's something that separates the interactions we have online with those in real life.

A weaker version of trust has emerged online in the past twenty years.

It's a shadow of what's expected in life offline.

It's not what it used to be.

It's almost deserving of a new definition: a lighter sort of trust, a Trust-Lite.

There's a version that has been crafted, accepted and then taken advantage of by tech companies.

Where has this taken us?

What have we lost in the process?

Who is pointing out this erosion?

Who is keeping silent?

And what's the next step?

*

To answer these questions we'll have to take a quick look at one of the greatest inventions of our tech-heavy age.

It's one that demonstrates just what is asked of us.

It's not the iPhone.

Rather, something even more important.

It's the latest incarnation of the terms and conditions.

In a politically divided time, one activity truly brings us all together.

No one sits down and reads the terms and conditions.

People used to.

Or at least they used to when they were at the bank, ready to sign a mortgage, or sitting across the desk from an insurance salesperson.

Small print was not a daily occurrence.

You paid attention when it came along.

Now we all refuse to scroll to the bottom.

We can't make that journey.

We don't read the T&Cs, the Privacy Policies (PP), the Terms of Service (ToS).

Whatever you want to call that onslaught of technical prose.

You've probably faced an update already today.

You've probably just blindly accepted some Ts and Cs.

We trust the companies that keep breaking our trust.

In 2017, Deloitte surveyed 2,000 consumers in the US. They found that 91 per cent of people consented to legally binding terms and conditions of service without reading them.

For those aged eighteen to thirty-four, a whopping 97 per cent agreed to conditions before even reading them.

In 2016, Jonathan Obar at York University in Toronto and Anne Oeldorf-Hirsch at the University of Connecticut conducted a study that upped the stakes even more.

They wanted to assess 'the extent to which individuals ignored Privacy Policy and Terms of Service when joining a fictitious social networking service, NameDrop'.

Taking the average adult reading speed of 250–280 words per minute, they figured it would take someone a mere 29 or 32 minutes to read the PP.

The ToS would take an additional 15 minutes of their day.

Unsurprisingly, they found people didn't want to read the fine print.

'Qualitative findings suggest that participants view policies as nuisance,' they wrote in their abstract, 'ignoring them to pursue the ends of digital production, without being inhibited by the means.'

The problem for the participants was that, as the academics phrased it, 'implications are revealed' down in that block of text.

And what implications they were.

As many as 98 per cent of participants missed NameDrop ToS 'gotcha clauses'.

These were the clauses that said they'd share users' data with the NSA and employers.

And, of course, users would have to provide a first-born child as payment for access to the social network.

> For the sake of those first-born children, I hope NameDrop
> is a terrific place to catch up with friends and make
> connections.
>
> Like!

*

Most of us would consider ourselves mildly suspicious, or at least unwilling to give away our first-born children.

But powerful techniques are honed to gain our trust.

In another study, two academics, Rainer Böhme of the University of California, in Berkeley, and Stefan Köpsell of Dresden's Technische Universität, looked at the wording of consent forms. They offered 80,000 participants alternative wordings of simple consent.

Some participants were mildly bullied – the kind of bullying in the Trust-Lite age we've become used to.

They were told their consent was required and then offered an 'I agree' button.

'They went along 26% more often than did other users, who had been politely asked to participate (with phrases like "we would appreciate very much your assistance" and both "yes" and "no" options represented by lookalike buttons),' wrote David Berreby in *The Guardian*.

When we're given the option to consider how much we should trust a company, some of us do make considerations and weigh the options.

But offering up our trust blindly has become the habit of the age.

We sigh, occasionally chastise ourselves, but go along with what has become habitual behaviour.

'Ubiquitous EULAs [end user license agreements] have trained even privacy-concerned users to click on "accept" whenever they face an interception that reminds them of a EULA,' Böhme and Köpsell wrote in their study.

There must be a solution.

There must be a way we can all work together.

Berreby ended his article by saying: 'Perhaps society could subject internet agreements to industry-wide codes of conduct. You don't have a contract with a doctor, but you can expect her to adhere to the Hippocratic oath . . .'

And sure, that could happen in a perfect world.

There are loose initiatives and blue sky thoughts.

What if there was an industry-wide agreement?

What if tech companies segmented their T&Cs?

What if a bubble popped up each time they wanted access to something new?

The terms could be presented to the user as and when they become relevant.

What if?

What's evident in the loose solutions bandied about is that they're built on a fragile stem of hope.

I've trusted this company blindly.

I hope they'll do the right thing.

(Cut to: Zuckerberg blinking in front of the cameras at the Senate hearings.)

*

The T&Cs reveal something about us: our laziness, our willingness to get to the good stuff, our willingness to hand over . . . whatever.

But they also act as revealing portraits of the companies themselves.

After all, this is the one interaction where some brutal honesty occurs.

In this interaction, there's no well-edited video with a soundtrack of plucked guitars.

There's no one dancing around to sell you the product or remind you we're better off connected.

It's legal text.

For companies that fetishize smooth surfaces, clean design, short sentences, simple messaging and bright colours, here's the spot where they get down to it.

In 2019, a journalist from the *New York Times* analysed the 'length and readability of privacy policies from nearly 150 popular websites and apps'.

Using a test to measure the complexity of the text, he found Facebook's privacy policy more difficult to read than Stephen Hawking's *A Brief History of Time*.

'Only Immanuel Kant's famously difficult *Critique of Pure Reason* registers a more challenging readability score than Facebook's privacy policy,' wrote Kevin Litman-Navarro.

The list is long, like a rap sheet.

In 2012, Instagram told its users they could now sell your photos to . . . whoever.

This was one instance where users suddenly cared about those T&Cs.

For a while.

Half the users left, but they seem to have all trickled back.

'TwitPic takes credit for your photos,' CNN reported on the now defunct firm, 'the company keeps your deleted images and you can't sue the company after a year.'

Even oldies but goldies like Sears and Kmart made a play back in 2007.

After offering participants a measly ten bucks to join their online community, they snooped.

They tracked users as they surfed the web, banked, checked up on prescriptions, and just lived their lives.

The justification was buried in the T&Cs.

Eventually, the retailer's parent company settled charges in 2009.

There's the invasiveness of Snapchat.

There's the way OnStar, the roadside assistance, would keep tracking your movement even after you cancelled the service.

Writers may think they're using Twitter as a real-time diary but guess who legally owns all those tweets?

My favourite, though, for the scope of the villainy of the T&Cs comes from the apps.

One stirring example was Brightest Flashlight Free app for Android.

Their brilliantly ignoble terms of service said the app would periodically collect information.

They didn't trust you, the user, enough to make it crystal clear they'd track your every move and deliver the information to third-party advertisers.

Most villainous of all was that you didn't actually have to accept.

The app began recording your whereabouts before you even offered your permission.

I sometimes envision these T&Cs personified.

They're villains who move undetected through the Trust-Lite society.

And when they all get together they can't believe how easy it's become to crack this societal safe.

Who knew all it would take was a block of legalese text?

It was like a skeleton key.

It would give you access to anything.

An example of this strange new devalued definition of the word 'trust' comes from the Apple T&Cs.

Apple is sleek in its messaging.

It carries the feeling of a company that should be trusted.

And we do trust it – we have to.

You don't get to become a trillion-dollar company by acting like a suspicious free Brightest Flashlight app.

But Apple T&Cs are the equivalent of a partner who just wants to know where you're at.

Look more closely.

This is just one facet of the Trust-Lite life.

*

Let's move from the fine print to the ratings.

What about how we view the forms we've trusted in the past?

We used to trust book reviews.

Now, authors sneakily write their own Amazon reviews, and their parents get in there as well.

We used to trust restaurant reviews.

Now, everyone knows Yelp can't be trusted because whingers and complainers flood the reviews, in a cloud of anger, after their meal arrives five minutes late.

We know this isn't the truth of a dining experience.

Ever seen a person grapple with a bad Airbnb review?

'They're talking about . . . me. My house. My life.'

We're used to viewing people through the prism of their Airbnb reviews.

We know what an Uber number means.

And then there's TaskRabbit and other personal service apps, and the much-bashed Peeple, the app that promised a way to rate everyone around you but, unsurprisingly, has yet to find much of a user base.

What happens to our interpersonal relationships and our expectations when we start relying on scores?

Our lives unfold, day-by-day, interaction by interaction.

We're constantly asked to enter our details, enter our new passwords, give secondary contact details, enter text in the box below.

Now that we've all bought into this ongoing process, there's not much choice other than to go along with it, say yes to the next update, click the box at the end of the most recent set of terms and conditions.

Trust is forced upon us.

Trust is demanded from us.

Trust accretes around us.

Its upkeep is important.

Does it wear us down to keep handing over so much personal data?

Are we getting tired of revealing so much for so little?

We have become dependent on this trusting environment.

But we've also become reflections of it.

Integers of trust.

We've become our unshakeable names.

I remember the first time I saw *The Crucible*.

It wasn't a particularly good production.

Lots of talk of witchcraft, not a lot of subtlety.

There's the moment when John Proctor decides to confess to engaging in witchcraft but refuses to sign the written confession the Judge wants to post on the church door.

Why?

'Because it is my name!' the actor bellowed. 'Because I cannot have another in my life!'

That line remains, even when bellowed, unvarnished and primal.

It's one of those moments – watch the Daniel Day-Lewis

version on YouTube – when raw exposition works, when a character's primal self is revealed.

But compared with today, John Proctor had an option.

Or, I should say, someone comparable, with a fast horse and an escape route, had an option – you could outrun your name.

Move a town or two away.

Reinvention was possible.

There were opportunities for a new start; the new town meant a chance to start over, to rebuild trust with a new group of people, to not be absolutely bound to the decisions of the past.

To remake one's name.

Look at the horror stories we tell ourselves now.

Is it too soon to turn to *Black Mirror* as a valid image?

The chills of the recent 'Nosedive' episode are derived from a nightmare scenario in which every human interaction comes with a rating.

The protagonist, Lacie, is a young woman living in a slightly amped-up version of our current situation.

The characters all live in a glib world of incessant, unstoppable ratings.

If Lacie was to give out a cry of 'But it's my name!' she'd be met by her peers with a shrug, because they're all aware of her name, and her rating – a lingering, overshadowing, overpowering number that strikes such fear in them all because it's simply the endpoint of all the other aggregates we've become so well versed in reading.

*

(We're all highly attuned to the meaning of ratings now.

One friend told me he used to be able to look at a wind pressure number and understand the conditions out on the ocean.

Now he spends more time looking at his Instagram likes.

He's developed a similar relationship with them.

He reads their meaning.

He understands the possible social weather conditions that lead to 54 likes instead of 78.)

It's a strange sort of boomerang.

We want to quantify and rate everything around us, we want trustworthy digits.

We want our movies – works of subtlety and ambiguity – to be turned into a cold percentage on Rotten Tomatoes.

But we also want to escape this beautiful system, this finely tuned machine.

We aren't inactive participants in this world of trust.

What's most terrifying about the *Black Mirror* episode is the unending nicety.

The world we've created doesn't turn off, won't give us a break.

The ratings system never stops.

'I feel like I've changed,' an Airbnb owner told me, not so long ago.

'I've become a performative version of myself.

'Trust me, trust me, trust me.'

She was late to pick up a young couple – that service was included – 'And I remember,' my friend said, 'the car ride back.

'It was so uncomfortable.

'Beneath all the performed niceties was this punitive undertone.

'I could tell they were angry and entitled and weren't particularly interested in accepting an apology.

'And sure enough, in rolled the negative review.

'So can people trust me?

'Does this ambiguity of the situation matter to an aggregation of reviews?'

And could this ever be changed?

The world of trust has expanded.

Proponents would say this is a very good thing.

Corporations are acting better.

People are acting better.

(Except they're both not.)

What's wrong with a little corrective?

If you're so worried about your name, don't do anything wrong.

We trust you'll do the right thing.

Is there a financial imperative to the trust we hand over?

My dad loves restoring cars.

It's one of his great passions in life.

Most enjoyable for him is the moment when he opens up the hood and finds out for himself what's wrong.

The garage sometimes offers good advice.

But he doesn't always trust those who work at the garage to

advise him, because sometimes they'll act hastily or misdiagnose the problem.

They're nice guys.

But they're driven by an ulterior motive.

Their immediate impulse is to tell him to replace a part.

This carburettor? Throw it away. Replace it.

Often, after returning from the garage, he'll suspect he might be able to fix the part himself.

At the very least he wants to take a look, weigh the options, judge the evidence.

Recently he bought an Alfa Romeo.

I sensed weariness in his voice when he told me about it.

'You open up the engine,' he said, 'and you can't really get to the engine. It's cordoned off. It's covered, encased.'

If you buy a Tesla, at some point that car is going to speak to you and let you know something is wrong and needs to be replaced.

You're going to have to trust that the system is making the right diagnosis.

This interaction is going to involve an act of trust on your part.

There is no way to eyeball it.

There's no way to appraise the evidence at hand.

A new battery might not be necessary.

An engine overhaul might not be the only remedy.

It's no secret the technological sensors we trust are tilted.

They're naturally tilted towards consumerism.

In 2017, Apple confirmed it intentionally slows down older

iPhones, 'a feature introduced last year to protect against problems caused by ageing batteries' reported *The Guardian*.

We trust our information won't simply be used to get us to
buy more.

We trust, we trust, we trust.

For many, a relationship with Amazon is an inescapable fact,
these days.

Our relationships with Amazon call for another type of
trust.

I was no different.

I trusted them blindly.

I had gotten to the point where I no longer looked up the
price of anything because the expectation is that Amazon is
going to be the cheapest.

If it's available from Prime and shows up the next day, it's a
double bonus.

It beats having to actually remove my credit card from my
wallet.

A while ago, I noticed I've just stopped looking at what my
daily needs cost.

A little while after noticing that, I questioned whether this
subservience to Amazon is healthy.

I'm blindly trusting Amazon to offer the best prices and I'm
losing any sense of the price of things.

It feels like I'm losing another skill.

We're losing the ability to question a company like Amazon.

We're losing the skill to discern.

*

We think of Amazon as an American company.

But I tend to think of them as a great Russian novelist.

Their ability to construct a psychological profile is far more intricate than Facebook.

Run through their research capabilities.

Alexa, the ranking engine, gives them all the global ranks of every website.

They own the overview of all traffic.

They're able to monitor the flows of history each day.

IMDb tracks and monitors what we're all watching, which gives them insight into tastes for Amazon Prime and Amazon Studios.

Goodreads was bought in 2013.

Why try to imagine what could possibly comprise a person's diet?

When you buy Whole Foods, you'll know.

In 2018 they acquired a small pharma company called PillPack.

The amount of insight is stunning.

These insights provide the broad strokes of the story.

But then look at the material we're submitting to them so they'll be able to plot out our own biographies.

My Amazon history discloses where I am in life.

These are not simply purchases, but predictive markers of the next chapter.

Amazon will know the month you stop buying tampons.

And if Amazon moves into pharmaceuticals – which has

been suggested – then the moment you stop buying Tampax you'll be suggested diapers. Or hormones.

Those who have long awaited this day are out there making noise.

Those who fear the machine in all its permutations are out there making noise.

What about those who think: It's handy. I enjoy it.

But I can't shake the feeling that there's a consequence to one company being given the ability to tell such a detailed story of a life.

Is this truly ease we're feeling?

Or is it intrusion?

Do we trust Amazon with the stuff of ourselves?

Just as we know writers and film-makers will push the way our stories are told, and experiment with form, so too will those who are telling our stories, these days.

It's not dangerous.

It's not malicious.

What I've noticed as the prevailing impulse in the tech world is: How far can I get with this?

There is push and retreat.

Boundaries are pressed against.

Pressure is exerted.

Is there any force that will stop Amazon at any point?

Where will that force come from?

What form will it take?

For companies, the challenge is evident and seductive.

I know, because my own company is ambitious in its own way.

A company embraces motion.

They will ask: Can I keep running?

And if they can keep running, and if they take over half the world, a company will ask: What do I do with it now?

A company like Amazon, guided by data, views us as characters with predictable needs.

In response, I'm starting to view them as a character.

To some degree, they've become a superhero.

They've got power that is now, at this point, difficult to wrest from them.

I feel jealousy, pride and respect for what they've achieved.

Like superheroes, a certain section of the populace is cheering them on.

We, as a populace, have enabled them.

As consumers, we've enjoyed.

But as human beings, I'm sensing worry.

And, in some cases, I'm feeling something more serious when it comes to my compatriots in the world of tech.

I feel betrayed.

I'm in a community and I don't see my own community living up to its 'best self', as they say.

I feel betrayed when I see Google brokering deals with China.

In Nick Bilton's *Hatching Twitter*, a gossipy recollection of those heady days when Twitter emerged, much is made of the anarchism, the coders who sit at the 'standing meeting' and stand when the boss asks everyone to sit.

Jack Dorsey's nose ring, the sake nights, the punk bands.

But somehow we got from there to what we have now.

I speak not as an outsider, but as someone in the world.

These were my heroes – at least, I, like others, bought into the early pronouncements.

I can still chart the progress, from thinking how unabashedly necessary it was for the forerunners of this generation to adopt 'Don't be evil' as a motto, all the way across the spectrum to that grim moment when that defunct phrase, peeled from the IIQ walls, became drenched in irony, not so long ago, when *The Intercept* broke news of Google's China plans.

My company is not perfect.

My ideas are not as slick as Malcolm Gladwell's.

I haven't read it all.

I'm not going to act like I'm in an amateur production of *Network*, go full Peter Finch and write the rest of the book in caps because I'M MAD AS HELL AND I'M NOT GOING TO TAKE THIS . . . etc.

Tech has been good to me.

It's been good to you, too.

It's not worth looking at what we've built in black and white.

In response to the hacking, the flood of fake news, Cambridge Analytica, the . . . I could go on, Facebook released a series of treacly, manipulative, sentimental ads that told us Facebook needed to get back to what it was all about.

And yes, of course, at that moment I said under my breath: 'Data scraping.'

But there was more to it, obviously.

The video made it clear the betrayal is not total.

There could be a way back.

What have we done to trust?

How can we go from Trust-Lite back to something more solid?

4: Big Data

A few years ago, at a MIT conference entitled 'Big Data: The Management Revolution', a technologist raised a couple of interesting points amidst the usual cheerleading.

Rachel Schutt was, at the time, a senior statistician at Google Research.

Amidst talk of Big Data euphoria, she stressed the importance of human traits like intuition and experience.

In a *New York Times* article about the conference she was asked what makes a good data scientist.

'Obviously,' she replied, when interviewed by reporter Steve Lohr, 'the requirements include computer science and math skills, but you also want someone who has a deep, wide-ranging curiosity, is innovative and is guided by experience as well as data.'

He ended his article with the following quote from Schutt, which seems to be the most important requirement: 'I don't worship the machine.'

*

I think about this viewpoint often when faced with the wonder and dread of Big Data, the catch-all description for huge data sets that can now be dissected to reveal patterns, trends, and associations.

It's increasingly important these days to forego worshipping the machine.

(The seductive machines we've built are easy to worship.)

At the same time it's increasingly important we all step up for a personal reckoning with the machine.

How do we appraise the issue of Big Data in our lives, especially if we don't have degrees in computer science?

Should we trust it without hesitation?

We're busy, we've got lives, we're pressed for time when asked to accept societal change.

We tick the terms and conditions, move along, all the while guided and goaded on by excited technologists.

It's a lot to handle.

It's a lot to visualize.

And the chatter has got louder on both sides.

Big Data is the Messiah, some shout out.

Actually, the other side says, visualize the Devil.

In that article about the MIT conference, it was interesting to see how much the humanities popped up.

It's going to be exceedingly important in the coming years, attendees pointed out, to examine the characteristics and ethics of Big Data.

It's going to become important to tell accurate stories with all this data we harvest.

Accurate stories.

Maybe we've got to be more poetic when we think of Big Data.
    If it's the Messiah, let's study each verse.
    If it's the Devil, should we list the details?
    We've got to find ways to make it present in our lives.
    We've got to look at how it's being described by others.
    Some say all these Big Data sets are just fuel, like so many cords of wood or stacks of coal, powering the furnaces of today.
    Who benefits from that inert description?
    What are Big Data's characteristics?
    Is it a presence?
    Is it looming?
    Is it a trustworthy system?
    An ever-expanding web?
    Is it both?
    What is Big Data to you?
    Is it a warm presence in your life?

Take it upon yourself.
    You, after all, are the provider.
    You will be working with the forces of Big Data, feeding it, living off its outcomes, for the rest of your life.
    If you haven't defined it for yourself, take a shot.
    The world of business and technology is already doing so.

*

One of the most common definitions is the most conventional.

At its most remedial, and at its most reassuring, Big Data is just the fuel that keeps a company running.

'Data really powers everything that we do,' said Jeff Weiner of LinkedIn.

Like many others, their furnace needs to be fed as the data they're collecting 'powers the algorithms behind suggestions for recruiters so they can find the ideal candidate, and for job seekers to find jobs that they may be interested in'.

For LinkedIn, this use of Big Data will obviously have a utopian endpoint.

Part of the vision is building on their existing offerings.

'So, imagine a world,' Weiner said, 'where every job and economic opportunity is digitally represented . . .'

Every job.

Among its many traits, Big Data helps big dreams come true.

Data is not just a fuel.

Data is becoming the new raw material of business.

'What we are seeing is the ability to have economies form around the data – and that, to me, is the big change at a societal and even macroeconomic level,' Craig Mundie, then head of research and strategy at Microsoft, said back in 2010.

Since then, Oracle, IBM, Microsoft and SAP have been pouring money into data management software firms

*

It's ambitious.

Perhaps we need to make our vision even larger.

Perhaps data sets are not just found *in* the world.

They *are* the world.

Over at a company called Factual, an information-sharing start-up, CEO Gil Elbaz asks us to imagine: 'The world is one big data problem . . . If all data was clear, a lot fewer people would subtract value from the world,' he says.

'A lot more people would add value.'

Elbaz, unsurprisingly, sees the world happily aided from every angle by Big Data.

Elbaz envisions a business world where, for instance, a restaurant chain would employ Factual to suss out a new location and ensure it's not too close to the competition.

They'd investigate ratings on Yelp, check for gas stations nearby to draw drivers off the highway, throw in a few other details.

The chain can also employ Factual to see where it is mentioned on the web, or to correct what other people are saying about it.

All this public data is fine.

Unsurprisingly, Elbaz goes further.

'Lately, I've been thinking that we need to get more personal data,' he told the *New York Times*.

'Big Data could use it all: genetic information, what they ate, when and where they exercised – ideally, for everyone on the planet, now and forever.

'I want to figure out a way to get people to leave their data to science.'

Big Data as tombstone.

A repository, endlessly expanding, taking in every movement of the living and compiling the stats of the dead.

The world as one big data problem – finally solved at the end.

For some, Big Data is an act of outright theft.

It's natural progression.

Big Data is inevitable.

Or maybe it's still the unknown.

'Big Data is like teenage sex,' said Dan Ariely, a professor at Duke University, 'everyone talks about it, nobody really knows how to do it, everyone thinks everyone else is doing it, so everyone claims they are doing it.'

It's the life-changing idea we've been waiting for, the evangelicals say.

It'll 'replace ideas, paradigms, organizations and ways of thinking about the world' predicted Erik Brynjolfsson, a professor and director at MIT, in 2012.

Look at the verb there: replace.

Because it's seen as such an active force, some posit we're in a new age.

A new force is acting upon us.

*

One computer scientist at the University of California, in Berkeley, Joe Hellerstein, believes we're in 'the industrial revolution of data', in the midst of incessant change that could be healthy or unhealthy.

We've heard the industrial revolution analogy before.
　　But this time the analogy should give us pause.
　　We're being pushed forward.
　　The revolution is happening around us.
　　The forward trajectory seems inescapable.
　　But at what cost?
　　This is why *now* is the time for appraisal – and self-appraisal, or disruption, is not something Silicon Valley or the greater world of tech is interested in perfecting.
　　We're going to need to do the work ourselves.

For me, Big Data is a form of storytelling.
　　Ultimately, it will create the new narratives, the new insights, call them what you like.
　　Big Data is a means to create narrative.
　　It gathers the stuff.
　　It shapes the story.

This means it provides the stories we're allowed to tell ourselves and others.
　　It's worth asking who is going to have the power to craft the narrative.
　　We've already witnessed the rise of the data scientist.
　　It's only the beginning.

A few years ago, *The Economist* described the data scientist as someone 'who combines the skills of software programmer, statistician and storyteller/artist to extract the nuggets of gold hidden under mountains of data'.

This statistician/storyteller will ensure some sort of alchemy occurs, some sort of meaning emerges, some sort of insight is found.

Before her botched run as presidential candidate against Donald Trump in 2016, Carly Fiorina had a few interesting things to say about the process way back in 2004, when she was CEO of Hewlett-Packard.

She announced a useful path from raw material to narrative.

The goal was to turn data into information, and information into insight.

'The issue is no longer where the information lives – what server, what application, what database, what data center.

'It's actually now all about putting information to work.

'It is about transforming data from passive to active, from static to dynamic – transforming data into insight.'

Hal Varian, Google's chief economist, predicted that the job of statistician will become the 'sexiest' around.

(I'd love to see a list of previous 'sexy' jobs.

The other example Varian provided was 'computer programmer in the noughties'.)

'Data sets,' he explained, 'are widely available; what is scarce is the ability to extract wisdom from them.'

Life is widely available.

What is scarce is the ability for a poet or novelist or film-maker to extract (and present) wisdom from it.

Transformation from source material to insight is the key here.

It's what we struggle with – and will struggle with, in times to come.

Big Data is expected to provide insight that is in itself unimpeachable narrative.

It must be right.

Insight is not: 'I think.'

It's: 'This is.'

But who gets to frame the insight?

And is it unimpeachably accurate, after all?

I haven't accepted that insight equals wisdom.

It's clear the data scientist will inherit a privileged role.

'We can't grow the skills fast enough,' said Claudia Perlich, chief scientist at Media6Degrees, an online ad-targeting start-up in New York.

It's an opportunity for kids.

Hal Varian says it might be time for our children to learn new life skills.

'The ability to take data – to be able to understand it, to process it, to extract value from it, to visualize it, to communicate it – that's going to be a hugely important skill in the next decades, not only at the professional level but even at the educational level, for elementary school kids, for high school kids, for college kids.

'Because now we really do have essentially free and ubiquitous data.

'So the complementary scarce factor is the ability to understand that data and extract value from it.'

The data scientist will be a sought-after job.

There are many risks involved.

There are many who would benefit from their own stories being told, or subverting the process to tell their own stories.

We could end up telling the wrong stories.

Giving the wrong interpretations.

Missing the point.

We've done it before.

The road from data to insight is perilous.

Thomas H. Davenport, the author of *Only Humans Need Apply: Winners and Losers in the Age of Smart Machines*, once said: 'A major part of managing Big Data projects is asking the right questions:

'How do you define the problem?

'What data do you need?

'Where does it come from?

'What are the assumptions behind the model that the data is fed into?

'How is the model different from reality?'

*

The process is not one of just feeding data into a furnace.

It's trickier.

'With too little data, you won't be able to make any conclusions that you trust,' said Douglas Merrill, former CIO/VP of Engineering at Google. 'With loads of data you will find relationships that aren't real.'

I pick through these interviews, listen to these voices, and keep thinking about those who are assuming the role of data scientist.

I think of the words of a guy named Alex Szalay, an astrophysicist at Johns Hopkins University, who is good at sounding the warning bell.

Worrying about the numbers is one thing.

What about the human element?

'People should be worried about how we train the next generation,' he warned.

'Not just of scientists, but people in government and industry.'

They'll be keen to tell their own stories.

We've always searched for specialists to give us wisdom.

We've always hungered for new ways – less mysterious, less elitist.

Here we are, ready to be told the greatest stories ever, drawn from complex mountains of gathered information.

Are we ready to receive wisdom from Big Data?

Or should we ensure there is an equally strong counter-narrative.

Personally, I'm ready to explore the compelling argument for lean data and responsible technology.

This kind of approach, writes Matti Keltanen in *The Guardian*, 'suggests starting with questions relevant to your business and finding ways to answer them through data, rather than sifting through countless data sets.'

It also means asking less of people.

These days, the story of Big Data told by the tech industry is always optimistic.

There's always a happy ending looming on the horizon.

What could ever go wrong?

Back at the MIT conference, 'Big Data: The Management Revolution', a panel was asked to cite examples of big failures in Big Data.

There was apparently a lot of silence in the room.

No one could really think of a tragic end to these myriad narratives.

Eventually, Steve Lohr reported, someone said that maybe the financial crash wasn't so good.

Eventually, the issue of false discovery popped up.

We're able to grab needles from an exceptionally large haystack.

The haystacks get bigger and bigger.

There's a problem.

Trevor Hastie, a statistics professor at Stanford University, was quoted as saying that 'many bits of straw look like needles'.

5: We Built this City

What's the internet to me?

Let's turn this ethereal, weightless concept into something real, something physical.

The internet is, after all, a physical presence.

Its tubes cross the ocean.

Its servers fill up deserts in Arizona.

Too often we're not prepared to visualize it in that way.

The photographer Trevor Paglen has done an essential project where he dives into the ocean and tracks the cables snaking along the sea floor.

He shoots portraits of Miami Beach (see overleaf), stressing the tranquillity and calmness of the scene, but look closer and you'll see the geo-coordinates of the underground cables.

The reality of the scene becomes apparent. This is the actual site where the internet exists.

It's a good idea.

I'd like the internet to become real to more people, especially since we're constantly told it exists on another plane.

We're told to live in the cloud: 'All your data is in the cloud.'
But the cloud has nothing to do with clouds.
There's nothing much cloudy about it.
It exists.
Your information moves from here to the mast, to a cable that is physically transferred through space, made of copper.
So let's not become too enamoured of the idea of a cloud.
Instead, let's tether this idea to the earth, to us, to the senses.
It's as real-world as you could possibly make it, yet we're not confronted with it. Caring about and fighting for a healthier internet is tough to visualize.
When it comes to climate change, people are prepared to march in the streets.
When it comes to pollution, people are willing to protest.
They're not yet ready to go to the streets to ensure the health of the internet.
Perhaps you have your own tangible, earthy analogy?
I see it as a city, a particular kind of city.
I call it a boomtown.

Boomtowns boom because they offer access to something valuable.
Often this resource looks limitless.
In our boomtown, Big Data flows from so many oil wells.
It's scraped from every section of our lives.
It could even be picked up by what look like inert mics.
Because it's omni-present, it must be infinite.

69

But no one knows when a boom is set to end.

Those in the industry sometimes criticize the analogy.

Of course, they say, this wellspring of data is not going to dry up; Big Data is going to power every decision we're going to make, going forward.

'If necessary, we're going to force people to give up the data because, well, we're in charge.'

(This is usually the voice of a developer.

This is the most visible example of how they can quickly switch from viewing the individual as citizen to the individual as commerce.)

The tech world are the guzzlers.

They're greedy.

They're addicted.

They're always going to want the machine to run faster and, in a way, they appear to be correct.

As a data provider, you won't dry up.

You won't stop creating data.

But in this boomtown, those gorging on the data surplus have not been taking into account a different brand of environmental movement.

People seem to be interested in pursuing a course of preservation – not so much a preservation of trees or landscape, but a preservation of the self.

It will be a minority.

It always is.

This minority will use a growing number of techniques that now include things like VPNs (virtual private networks), private browsing and ad blockers.

The mass will pay for convenience over security – there's no arguing otherwise – but a few people seem to be interested in turning the nozzle.

Like any vanguard movement, people who don't want things to happen can bring about change.

*

Once a boomtown has been built, it exists.

You either raze the place or try to work with the infrastructure that already surrounds you.

Recreation of this particular boomtown is not possible.

After all, what are we going to do?

Tear down the entire internet?

Instead, we can look at cities for another option.

From within the existing structures, we can figure out a way to make this place work again.

Look at the existing map of the internet.

You're constantly living in the world of Google.

You live in the nation of Apple.

There's the land of Facebook abutting it.

They are the great real-estate developers of this place.

We're never going to buy back all that land.

Instead, we've got to look for the reclaimed space.

When I survey that map and come close to despair, I like to think of the example of the High Line, an elevated park and greenway that runs for about a mile and a half above the streets of New York.

It wasn't created from nothing.

It wasn't built from new materials, but rather constructed

on a former New York Central Railroad spur on Manhattan's west side.

Some people say it's just a railroad track with planters and trees on it, affording people a view of the meat packing district.

But look at it as something more.

View it as an example of reclaiming space in a place where that act is often improbable, if not impossible.

The High Line emerged from an urge to redevelop obsolete infrastructure as public space.

'We're gonna take this over and we're gonna turn it into something else.

'Something we need.

'Something that is actually going to bring and connect and give us space that doesn't exist.'

All of that happened within the framework of an existing city – and a city not so friendly to the idea of using space for the public good rather than private gain.

Within a city like New York, it's a story of determination.

A non-profit group urged the process along, and yes, it did get support from some high-flying New Yorkers like Diane von Furstenberg and Barry Diller, but there was also a great moment when an artist reminded people the High Line was not an abstraction.

Photographer Joel Sternfeld's photos showed viewers its physical reality and potential.

The story is attractive because it's not a typical New York tale of 'I made a lot of money so I bought a plot of land and I put up the biggest skyscraper I could.'

It happened in the place where you'd expect the opposite.

I like to apply this lesson to the internet, because we too are dealing with a pre-existing structure.

The city's already there.

So how are you going to improve it, navigate through it, find corners of reclamation?

We can accept the boomtown for what it is, and then try to build upon it.

Just as the High Line happened in a mature city, we can make changes as the internet matures.

We can choose to live better within the existing framework.

Once we accept the internet as a physical place, we might have more empathy for those around us.

We're going to have to start reframing the way we look at the worth of these streams of data coming out of the ground; we're going to have to realize the stuff of our lives is what is being used to develop AI, to fortify companies that already have a stranglehold on us; we're going to have to change our thinking.

Maybe we'll have to adopt a more mercenary view of the stuff of our lives.

If these companies have taken up so much space, if they're using us as their raw material, perhaps they should pay.

Eduardo Porter noted in the *New York Times*, in March 2018: 'Getting companies to pay transparently for the information will not just provide a better deal for the users whose data is scooped up as they go about their online lives.

'It will also improve the quality of the data on which the information economy is being built.'

And, he points out, it's only going to become more important.
We live in this place but we don't ask for anything.
Even if we could, what would we ask for?
People have obviously benefited.
But are they sure of what they're being paid?
The offline analogy would be a supermarket with no prices on anything.
Is your data worth $1 or $99?

So what will this improvement look like?
There are a few different options.
My chosen path leads, unsurprisingly, from my own experience.
To give you a sense of our inadvertent success, I need to go back and explain how WeTransfer came about.
We're going to need to go to Holland.

PART TWO

Envisioning the Solution

The WeTransfer Story (My Story)

6: In the Beginning

In 2009, there were a lot of bloggers out there and, amongst them, a few blogging superheroes: fast-talking Gary Vaynerchuk with all his tips and 'how tos'; Mashable's Pete Cashmore, who busted out of Aberdeenshire, Scotland, as a nineteen-year-old in 2005; Arianna Huffington and her endless sprawl of content.

In his 2006 book *An Army of Davids*, Glenn Reynolds argued that markets and technology empowered ordinary people to beat Big Media.

A platoon of people had formed online, and there they were, fighting the Goliath.

I'd heard of a certain 26-year-old who was valiantly wielding his keyboard.

Nalden was a blogger. If you were tech literate and interested in design (in Holland) you knew him. You knew his taste. He was young, he had boundless energy, but he didn't necessarily know the ways of the world. He was green – nearly translucent – from spending too many hours in windowless rooms, bent over with the posture of Neanderthal man, his days of productivity spent staring at a backlit screen, hunched over a wireless keyboard.

He'd talk to you when he detached from the internet, but that crucial moment was rare. He wore a deerstalker, and because of his baby face, the outfit meant he shared a glowing resemblance to Elmer Fudd.

I was drawn to him. At the time, I had my own reasons for seeking out interesting people who wore deerstalkers, people who weren't so embedded in my own industry. In the midst of what now seems a repulsive and unhealthy globetrotting phase, I was busy jumping on planes like they were buses.

Much to my wife's discontent, I spent a few days each week away from Amsterdam, in Moscow and London.

The world of advertising had seemed dazzling and adventurous in the early days of my career when I was working for Stella McCartney and BBDO. But quick trips here and there, face-to-face meetings that didn't go anywhere, and products I didn't believe in, were beginning to take their toll.

If Nalden was green, I was starting to look a similar shade, and at the time had managed to lose 16kg from stress and lack of sleep. Not even the heavy Russian food helped. These days, even the slightest smell of dill in a soup or scattered across a plate will catapult me back to Domodedovo Airport in Moscow. My work–life balance had toppled to one side. It was a fortuitous time for us to cross paths.

Nalden poked his head into my office one day. He was wearing his deerstalker. I'm sure he said a few words, but he mostly laughed, or cackled, as that tends to be his preferred mode of conversation: a joyous cackle. We clicked. He was looking for something new, something bigger than his current projects, something more important. I told him I was feeling the same impulse.

We chatted about the internet, advertising, PR, his blog nalden.net, for which he was well known. We discussed a guy called Bas, who had started an interesting service called Oy Transfer. With the help of Nalden, the Oy had become We – a crucial tweak for the non-Dutch of the world – and WeTransfer had gone on to start disrupting the file transfer space, mostly because of one attribute: the simplicity of the design.

I don't think either of us realized that this was a beginning of sorts. He was excited at the possibility of global travel, bigger problems to solve, more money, and growth. I was excited at the prospect of starting a project for myself again. I'd get to decide what got me out of bed each day. I'd get to choose where to spend my time. This might lead to taking fewer flights, but also to a more satisfying connection to the world, a chance to engage with the most important ideas of the time.

Trust was already one of those important ideas.

7: Money

The beginning was a necessary scramble. Nalden was work-ing for nalden.net. WeTransfer was in its larval stages. The file transfer world was in flux. I wasn't getting much satisfaction from advertising. And, at the core of it all, there wasn't really any money lying around in Amsterdam. Not real money.

WeTransfer: no money.

Nalden's blog: not much money.

European tech in general: not exactly handing out cash hand over fist.

Large European banks don't tend to invest in early-stage tech, so new life for any new company is tough, certainly tougher than for our Californian counterparts.

But still, you've got to keep pressing onwards.

At the time, we thought there was a space in the market for a new sort of company – one that would incubate ideas and potentially serve as a bridge from the simplicity and creativity of nalden.net to the effective and reliable gesture at the core of WeTransfer.com.

Like most start-ups, money was of the utmost importance

to us. How would we live, how would we thrive? Should we take money from venture capitalists? What were the upsides and downsides? Was Europe the right place to be for us? I had two kids. Even at the age of two, they had a thorough understanding of the difference between wool and cashmere.

In Europe, there is some money available, but generally at a premium. There are instances of companies raising considerably more, but those deals will usually garner front-page news. For instance, the AR company Layar, founded to augment data on to your camera viewfinder, raised $14 million in 2010. It was listed as a digital pioneer at Davos, featured in *Wired* and *TIME* magazine and was the darling of the Dutch tech world for a time.

It's not unusual for any entrepreneur to speak to between thirty and forty investors. Certainly at the time WeTransfer was starting out, many of the people we knew were endlessly seeking funding, sometimes finding cash, often failing.

No one wants to take the sort of chances venture capitalists take in North America.

Still, we tried not to be dissuaded. At the time we held firm to our belief that there was a space in the market for a new sort of company. A company that could be the hub for a type of advertising model that worked in this new age.

This minor innovation was very important to us, even from the beginning.

The new model would not be based on Big Data, intrusion or irritation, but would instead be a radically transparent throwback. Already, at this point, we felt the intrusion and data mining that was an increasing feature of the online experience was only going to get worse. So, we decided to go with our instincts. We'd be up front with people. As people transferred files, we'd utilize the full screen.

Our pioneering move was done inadvertently. We just knew it felt good at the time.

The file transfer market was not, as they say, in a good place. RapidShare and MegaUpload were the mainstays. Their business model was based upon piracy, or throttling, which is as pleasurable as the term sounds. People flocked to their sites to illegally download the latest movie, and whilst the customer was there, the sites bombarded them – like some sort of spamming machine gun – with useless banner ads.

We wanted nothing to do with them. We certainly didn't want to compete with them. Our hope was to differentiate through quality and a respect for creativity.

If you're too young to remember the old days of file sharing, I'll help paint a picture of one of the most infamous examples of the industry: Kim Schmitz or Kim Tim Jim Vestor, otherwise known as Kim Dotcom.

Kim was arrested for hacking in 1994. He started file sharing business MegaUpload, a site that was shut down in 2012 for copyright infringement, reportedly costing copyright owners $500 million.

He didn't need to raise any money from external parties. He was a master at raising it himself. After fleecing people in 2002 with LetsBuyIt.com, he was reportedly earning $110,000 a day in 2010 from MegaUpload.

Today he resides in New Zealand, in Queenstown's most expensive leased property, facing extradition back to the US.

Because we couldn't raise money, we had another strategy – and it wasn't pornography or copyright theft.

Our money-making venture would run alongside WeTransfer and would be called Kuuva.com. We created a service that would stream art directly to your desktop screensaver or wallpaper.

This had potential because we believed that people would pay a premium to spend time in front of quality, curated backlight instead of the stock images Microsoft and Apple provided at the time.

Over time we believed we would be able to encourage some of the world's premium advertisers to join, and thus we would be able to monetize the service.

Nalden agreed to start this other company alongside everything else. We'd build a platform filled with great artwork and advertising.

It would obviously – why think small? – fulfil its role as the future of advertising. We would build a fan base centred around the user's love of art, and pay for the service by serving beautiful ads in between art.

We'd also started a design company, Present Plus.

A few weeks later, we convinced Nike to become one of the first clients within Present Plus. Nike would help us to finance this new venture and act as a showcase for our new advertising model.

They felt the time was right. There was a general backlash against the bitty intrusiveness of online advertising, with the forward-thinking employees of different companies beginning to seek out alternatives. Somewhere in these boardrooms, there was at least one voice saying: 'Maybe we should stop it with these banner ads.'

The full-screen ad was a mildly bold gesture.

It wasn't going to solve world hunger but it was going to, at the very least, hark back to the full-page advertising of Katie Grand's *POP* magazine and the *New York Times*, when photographers and graphic designers knew they'd have a chance to make a statement. Nike agreed to try and work with us on a concept around full-screen advertising, outside of any of their own platforms.

At this point Bas and Nalden had asked me to join WeTransfer. I couldn't say no, but I worried about what I had gotten into as soon as I said yes.

It was a complicated time. We had two offices, multiple products. We were hustling, trying to weave the strands together.

At WeTransfer we set forth to build up the service and ensure that, at the very least, files would keep getting transferred, time and time again. Why were we doing it this way? It all came back to money, as it usually does. Money was a pressing issue – and access to it is not equal, from one time zone to the next.

Raising the stuff in the Netherlands is not like raising money in Silicon Valley. To raise $200,000 in 2010 would probably have meant giving away 20 to 30 per cent of the business. The option was there, but just the prospect of offering up so much for so little made us queasy. That was not a deal we were willing to make. We didn't trust what we'd get in return.

So what do you do when you're trying to maintain control

of your company in the midst of a particularly painful episode of bootstrapping? At the time, consulting seemed to be the way out for us. It would mean juggling projects, but doing all this work ensured we'd be able to maintain control. We all agreed that control was important. And it wasn't a chore to consult. A project for a large brand that lasts for two or three months can often yield as much as $150,000. If you're lucky, a whopping 50 per cent is margin.

We could give away a chunk of the fledgling business, or we could just keep our heads down. It was much easier to consult and work two jobs than do the moneymaking rounds in Amsterdam.

We certainly weren't in Silicon Valley. We knew that much.

Holland is a trading nation. You can very easily start a business that buys cheap hotel rooms and sells them at a 10 per cent markup. You can start a denim brand that buys fabric at $3 per m² and sells it for $120 a pair of jeans. It's ten times harder to convince a tradesman to invest in a cultural business. And all the activities we were involved in, in some shape or form, encompassed design, art, community, film or culture.

We had to offer something real. The Dutch can trust the reality of a hotel room – it exists in space – or the reality of the fabric that will soon become an overpriced pair of jeans. Even at this early stage, we had to stress trust. Even though we were trafficking in file transfer and culture, we couldn't just present business ideas on the back of an envelope.

It couldn't be all blue sky, all the time.

Coming from this culture meant that we could bring some of its straight-shooting values into the online world. Would a

Dutch enterprise act like MegaUpload and spam a user into submission? Maybe not. Instead of fighting against the culture of our home country, we decided to embrace it.

We'd go Dutch, so to speak.

8: Find Your People

In the beginning, WeTransfer was small. We were six people gathered in a room – or two rooms – on the second floor of a converted canalside house in Amsterdam. It had once been the apartment of an old opera singer. The floors were cheap laminate. There was a green built-in bookshelf and only three desks in this mothballed studio flat.

Even back in its embryonic state, all sorts of people recognized that WeTransfer was going to be *something*. Those who made contact with the interface used the service. They clicked on a background. Others questioned our growth, the business model and our desire to change the online advertising business.

In February 2010, we were managing 47,000 transfers per week. By January 2011, we were up to 574,182 transfers per week and for the whole year grossed just €210,000 income.

Our salary costs were low, but the costs of running the small number of servers we had parked in Haarlem were beginning to escalate. It seems like a drop in the ocean today, but €20,000 per month in hosting costs felt like a stupidly large amount of capital outlay.

One day, early on in the life of WeTransfer, we got a sense of how quickly things were progressing. In London, Nalden and I walked past the offices of *It's Nice That*, a publication we both respected. We decided to knock on the door and introduce ourselves.

We sheepishly walked inside, met the founders Will Hudson and Alex Bec and told them we were over from Amsterdam. We were huge fans. We loved their brand and wanted to show our appreciation. They were flattered, very polite and friendly. They kindly reciprocated and asked what we did. When we said we were from WeTransfer, their response was immediate: *'No fucking way!'*

'Hey,' they summoned the team from the back of the studio to come out. 'These guys are from WeTransfer.'

Nalden and I looked at each other. We had no idea the business had such reach. We had no idea the business was so recognizable and appreciated. We had no idea these guys would respond with such enthusiasm.

Why? The answer was easy.

We soon realized a typical WeTransfer user profile was emerging: creative and involved in tech but not necessarily card-carrying members of the tech world, people who cared about design, cared about being in an artistic community (and yet still wanted to use a product that worked). The more we poked around, the more we began to discern the communities, the groups, the webs of people who used the product. It would be a blanket statement to say they all had uniform beliefs, but an identity had formed.

From small user studies, through feedback to our support

teams and later through larger outsourced quantitative and qualitative analysis, we were clearly differentiating ourselves from the competition through creativity; designers, film-makers, musicians and especially photographers loved us.

Mostly, we heard from people that they felt respected. We weren't pestering them, so they felt an allegiance to us. These early voices were important. They confirmed our hunches.

Around this time there were more and more people getting fed up with the competition. They were fed up with sign-up forms, with the complexity and instability of FTP, with USBs, hard drives, YouSendIt. Users loved that we allowed them to focus on creating rather than worrying about delivery. We were already trusted. Though people were discussing WeTransfer, no one quite knew the limits of possibility. We knew this was just the beginning.

So what's the key here? Find your people is the golden rule.

Find a group of people, and influence each other, learn from each other's values. This was another inadvertent lesson we learned: ensure you listen to users – not just on the subject of what's working and what's not, not just on how the service can grow and be tinkered with, but get a sense of their needs. In our case, we went even further and got a sense of our users' fears. This is usually territory tech companies don't want to visit – often because their own ambitions clash with the fears of their users. Users become wary of the behaviour and tactics of the services they're using. (This is how the hate-use internet arises.) In hindsight, our consultations led to a lot of discussions around what people were already scared of, and what they were beginning to fear.

Running a company that depends on constant interaction yields fascinating ongoing insights into the lives of people. Some companies believe the best way to act is to secretly monitor these interactions. For us, the consultations weren't secret. We heard from people, heard them loud and clear, heard about everything from the mental toll that comes from dealing with pop-up ads to the glory of feeling like you weren't being taken advantage of. We began to hear from designers and creative individuals who lived their entire days trading information on WeTransfer, and this process was only possible because the service did not intrude in this give-and-take of information. And, we were told, there was ease without monitoring. Ideas, we were told, felt safer in transit through our services.

One of the greatest fears in the creative process is ideas being made vulnerable. Some users, we were told, were starting to distrust Google.

This wasn't data that could be instantly turned into a profit. These weren't insights that could be compiled, but we chose to listen to this persistent push of anecdotal evidence. It was a way of monitoring and comparing our own fears. Companies have fears too. Were we being good enough to users? Were we being too good? Should we give in and become more rapacious? Who were we responsible to? What is responsibility?

Much is made of the growth of start-ups. The mythology of the start-up is documented again and again – white guys pounding on laptops, chugging Soylent, *Hatching Twitter*, you've heard it all before. These narratives are obsessed with scenes of fundraising, of sticking it to the VCs. Who didn't love the Zuckerberg-in-a-bathrobe scene in *The Social Network*? But the growth of some start-ups, ours included, also incorporates the growth of values. There are sometimes intense push-pulls within a company. Growth includes the reactions of the human beings on the outside, who begin to trust the company, work with the company, invest their time in using what we've got to offer. There are the moments when a user makes a hellishly good point that keeps us on our toes. There are the threats: 'If you guys ever change, we're out of here. If WeTransfer ever starts to intrude, if the feel shifts, we're gone.'

In this back and forth, we found our people. Our people found us. As that dialogue grew, we heard from them what they need – what some of them craved. As the era of data mining came upon us, we heard voices that carried more emotion. 'We need a place to turn to,' users told us, with more desperation than back in 2010. These scenes are not as easy to dramatize, but in this era of surveillance it's important for companies to talk about this part of the story. Does the story include a section where a company gathers up what's being said about it and decides we've got to listen to these people? Or does a company close the door and say, *sotto voce*, we've got to take advantage of these people?

These people. They're your people.

I'm glad we found a group. A group that will let us know if we've done them wrong.

9: To Go Big or Not to Go Big?

Back in 2010, we engaged in endless discussions about the use of data. At the time, Big Data was the hot topic. People like the amazingly talented David McCandless, a data journalist and one of the most respected information designers around, were making data sexy.

Every company bragged about knowing more and more about its users. All over the world, data architects, analysts, experts were getting pumped by the likes of Oracle, IBM, Microsoft and SAP, whilst Facebook was under fire for knowing too much, for claiming the rights to information people had unwittingly offered up. Instagram claimed copyright over imagery. In general, the market was frantically drawing up infographics to brag about their knowledge.

And oh, the bragging. Oh, the infographics. To be caught in the dull-eyed, evangelical stare of a data scientist talking about Big Data was something to behold.

Their words worked. Every company feared being left behind. The fear was palpable. If you were not part of the new data extraction industry, what were you left with? How soon did you want to die? It was like you'd shown up in the boomtown and were sitting lacing up your shoes while prospectors staked their claims, drove in their pickaxes. *Why are we not doing this?* There were voices in most organizations asking this question, sometimes in a considered manner, sometimes shrill. It's a tough question to answer.

We asked ourselves if we should use more of our collected data to target users. At that time, we had only gathered hundreds of thousands – rather than millions – of users. Should we start looking at who was using the service? Should we investigate their actions? Could we? What sort of data could be gathered? Much of this conversation was driven by the fact we were bootstrapped. Energy rich – cash poor. We weren't looking for investors. We were just trying to get the business off the ground.

In the end, we agreed we would ask ourselves a simple question: 'What would we like to obtain from our users?' The resounding answer was: 'Nothing. We should try to protect our users.' We knew our community. We'd heard them express their fears.

Our goal, we decided, should be to create a safe haven for people to get stuff done. It was that simple. Again, this sentiment seems at first glance straightforward but it has become inadvertently revolutionary in this industry. Users shouldn't have to worry about where their data is being stored. They shouldn't worry about it being misused. So that's what we did: nothing.

(As an aside, one of the problems with the business book industry is it's very tough to be able to preach stasis, to tell people to do nothing. Businesses thrive on action, Top 10s, or so we're told. Better to be a bold decision maker (and be totally wrong) than be too ponderous, too slow to act. Better to move fast, and break things of value and worth and irreplaceable cost, than do nothing. But, in fact, here we are, and here's the lesson we learned: doing nothing is sometimes a strong move.)

We try to hold the same beliefs today as we did back then. It's not always easy. External pressure never relents. Since we launched Collect for iOS and acquired Paper, the drawing app for iOS, the fight to hold on to our core beliefs has become more challenging. As soon as you're running apps across the app store and offering multiple products, this becomes more complex.

Retrospectively, you could call this our inadvertent 'small data policy'. We use the minimum data necessary to ensure we can serve uber-premium ads to the right people in order to keep offering a free service to the other users.

The right people being those who cared, those spending enough time on the internet to call it their workplace, and those who especially appreciated our attention to detail and desire to remain focused and in a state of flow.

To quote Ken Robinson: 'Flow, also known as the zone, is the mental state of operation in which a person performing an activity is fully immersed in a feeling of *energized focus*, full involvement and enjoyment in the process of the activity.'

For a while we've employed terms that are now creeping into vogue: humanistic, authentic, lean, responsible, culture-driven.

Although we are a technology company, we want to apply technology and innovation to the product without compromise. That means we don't have to compromise. Users don't have to compromise.

I don't know exactly how we've done it but we've been able to grow, and when I look back, the outcome of ushering a company forward in a fraternal environment means that we've been able to relate to our users in a different way.

And actually I do know how we've been able to grow.

We've moved from 1 million files transferred per day in 2012 to 1 billion files transferred per month in 2018, with transfers taking place in 195 countries and nearly every major fashion brand in the world advertising on the site.

That came about because we've been able to ask questions like: 'How should we relate to our users?'

Our experience from initiating a constant conversation with our users paid off. We didn't need to relate to them in one, monolithic way. We didn't have to set up an antagonistic relationship. They weren't seen as people we had to dupe. We're not their owners. We're not their Facebook friends.

Companies tumble forward, some grow and some, like Facebook, expand into businesses so strapping and large they need to keep redefining their relationships and redefining themselves as they get bigger and bigger. Perhaps it's the nature of Facebook itself, or the personality of its creator, but this great tech presence seems to say it knows what's best. It's not the only one.

Lean data means you don't have to do this. A lean data policy means you're able to progress using the same definition of the word transparency that we, as human beings, have been using for centuries.

On the other hand, a company like Facebook is all about a brand-new definition of transparency – the transparency of our time, and not just the common or garden variety but something that borders on 'radical transparency'. Transparency that's expected from you, the consumer, but never from them, the folks at Facebook.

'You know what's good for you? We'll tell you. We'll let you know.'

We knew this was not the kind of paternalistic relationship we wanted with users.

One example: 'You know what's good for our users?' Facebook seemed to say. 'Not having a different personality at work than at home.' But was this real transparency?

'Even if we don't intend our secrets to become public knowledge,' writes Franklin Foer (on the subject of the wants of tech in his recent book *World Without Mind*), 'their exposure will improve society. With the looming threat that our embarrassing information will be broadcast, we'll behave better. And perhaps the ubiquity of incriminating photos and damning revelations will prod us to become more tolerant of one another's sins.'

Yeah. Perhaps.

Or perhaps we should just let people be.

Besides, Foer goes on to say, there's virtue in living our lives truthfully, right? We're told that. By Facebook. Could anything be more paternalistic than Facebook's ongoing attitude towards us?

Foer likens it to the technologists' view – Zuckerberg has unknowingly become heir to the tradition of engineers knowing what's best.

At a certain point, we looked at our own company and made a decision – and it was easy to make – that the way we'd relate to our users was not Zuckerberg-paternalistic. We'd been amongst them, in the middle of them, in the beginning, and we'd continue to work alongside them. And we'd find a way to show this was viable.

A social network is very different from a sharing system, some would argue. Sure, but we're both providing free tools to enable connection, and we're both meeting users at an intersection where they could possibly offer up personal information. We could use them or we could work with them. As we progress, we must see this meeting point as a chance for definition. And it's worth offering up a viable alternative option.

We need to make it clear that within the world of Facebook, you will be told. It's not exactly a circle of empathy. The decisions born out of a technocratic impulse are made for you, and the reality of working and creating within Facebook, or the worlds of Google, means entering spaces where the opaque algorithms can affect you and decide what's right. In the Facebook world you are given what seems to be great power, but is that true? Look at the flow of thought. The flow of a feed. The flow of information for Facebook is not unimpeded. It's manipulated.

It may be the sort of action a company would use with an underling. But what about a co-worker?

For us, in a more modest way, the idea of file transfer is the beginning of a clear, non-opaque relationship. It's a start. It's a gesture. We work alongside you, and this sense of being at the user's elbow, rather than somewhere above them, needs to emerge as an alternative. More than anything, this is a tone we set early on in our growth, and it will follow us – a process where we are not telling someone what to do.

However big WeTransfer gets, we will be able to offer an experience that does not obstruct. How do we fund this? Can we use these tools in a better way? Can we grow a tech business that doesn't rely on the dark arts? And by extension, can all of you next-generation, hot-stepping start-uppers do the same?

I often wonder if it's time to fuse the online and offline worlds together. Decades into the life of the internet, might it be time to bring the ethos of companies like Patagonia and Ben & Jerry's into the online world? There must be money to be made by adopting the ethos of companies that operate in a different way than that easy villain, Facebook.

Maybe adopting offline values will take an ongoing education for the consumer. Maybe such values will be introduced by employees who are getting tired of the questionable morals of tech companies.

Maybe Facebook employees will tire of feeling like hackers and might recognize themselves as being on the wrong side of the fight for civil rights (and in this case that could be shorthand for privacy rights).

Not everyone will suddenly be virtuous – what are the freaking odds? – but this promise of a more symbiotic world/

work experience is becoming more seductive – and necessary. Adopting and repurposing offline values means using the great and powerful tools of tech without an underlying tone of manipulation.

It's coming.

Maybe the consumer will have to lead. People are beginning to realize something's wrong. You don't have to taste the pesticides. Sometimes it's enough to be told they're on your foods.

In the past, what has happened next?

You change your behaviour, and look for companies that are working with you, rather than against you. Information companies, companies that distribute information, companies that could, with no questions asked, demand more personal data – we're entering a time when two-way transparency is necessary. Offline values are necessary.

Transparency is not solely expected of the user.

10: What the Hell Do You Do if Everyone's Doing Big Data?

These days, if you're in business, you're probably going along with Big Data. You've probably been told of its importance by the high priests of tech. You've been both scared and awed by its reach. Scared of missing out and a little worried about going down the path and becoming a true believer.

Now might be a good time to elaborate more on this idea of lean data or responsible tech. Call it our inadvertent business strategy. It's never going to be as big as Big Data – hence its leanness. Let's get that out of the way at the beginning. We're not stuffing the Big Data genie back in the lamp.

But Big Data should not be confused with all data.

For as long as WeTransfer has existed, the large companies around us have been talking about Big Data. Big Data was going to be the saving grace of mankind, as we would be able to deliver exactly what people wanted exactly when they wanted it.

It was rightly celebrated. It was, in that unfortunate phrase, a 'game changer'. But the phrase 'Big Data' was often yelled out in a way that seemed creepily evangelical. Tech people have, I've noticed, a tendency to sound like unhinged preachers when it comes to the latest find.

The fact that it was an uphill struggle was evidenced by the lack of interest from the majority of major advertisers and media companies because of our lack of data. Because of our inability to target, re-target and profile. Unlike many, we were unable to predict your menstrual cycle. It would take a maverick within an organization, who possessed that rare ability many in media don't have, to be able to listen to and take a punt on WeTransfer and allow us to make him a local hero, by demonstrating the power of design over data.

The sheer arrogance of the IAB (institute of advertising standards), who refuse to recognize us as a standard format, to this very day, is a demonstration of how we are still being seen as an outsider or challenger, despite our scale.

The contempt we were shown by many of the big media conglomerates when presenting our wares, as 'they simply couldn't recommend us' – we were often told: 'We'll try, perhaps X brand has some experimental budget we can find?' – led us to think we'll do this on our own. So we did.

And then there were the investors, who would look down their noses at us, as they weren't able to model without that data. I'm sure no one could model the Model T when Henry was busy revolutionizing the world.

In the mighty emerging world of Big Data, the act of searching for a nearby waffle restaurant could very well be a step towards understanding the secrets of mankind, bit by bit, imprint by imprint.

'The everyday act of typing a word or phrase into a compact, rectangular white box leaves a small trace of truth that, when multiplied by millions, eventually reveals profound realities,' Seth Stephens-Davidowitz announces in his book *Everybody Lies: Big Data, New Data, and What the Internet Can Tell Us About Who We Really Are.*

'Let me be blunt,' he goes on. 'I am now convinced that Google searches are the most important data set ever collected on the human psyche.'

For Stephens-Davidowitz and others, the value of Big Data is its ability to collect data that would otherwise never see the light of day. It would normally lie around untapped, never be admitted or spoken aloud to the world at large.

'At the risk of sounding grandiose,' he says, 'I have come to believe that the new data increasingly available in our digital age will radically expand our understanding of humankind.'

Its proponents are not only enamoured of the amount of data but also what can possibly be considered data. For people like Stephens-Davidowitz, there's no limit. Take sex. There's so much data on porn now, the stuff is of the quality 'Schopenhauer, Nietzsche, Freud, and Foucault would have drooled over'.

Most importantly, this data is, in his word, 'honest'. Others have used different ways of describing it. This is 'dark data', an untapped landscape of the soon-to-be-quantifiable. Believers hint at limitless reach and no reason to ever stop collecting and collecting.

'In the pre-digital age,' Stephens-Davidowitz writes, 'people hid their embarrassing thoughts from other people. In the digital age, they still hide them from other people, but not from the internet . . .'

It's the ultimate truth-teller. The implication here is that we should delve deeper and deeper and deeper, but not to worry: there will be a separation. Big Data will harvest all this honest data – and by 'honest' we mean our most intimate revelations. But 'other people' won't find out. 'Big Data allows us to finally see what people really want and really do, not what they say they want and say they do.'

The excitement is always palpable when reading the writings of the evangelical believers. It's often difficult to find any downside, any threat, any hint of a shadow. In the scenario above there remains some sort of well-policed divide between data and identity. This barrier, it's implied, will be there to keep us safe. But who is manning that barrier? Is that the barrier whose security and strength is being protected by Facebook, the notorious bastion of unhackable safety? By Google?

As the evangelical word of Big Data spread, I started to notice the way its proponents were excited by their own insatiability. Everything could become data. Everything was already data. Light data, dark data.

'These days, a data scientist must not limit herself to a narrow or traditional view of data,' writes Stephens-Davidowitz, 'These days, photographs of supermarket lines are valuable data. The fullness of supermarket bins is data. The ripeness of apples is data. Photos from outer space are data. The curvature of lips is data. Everything is data!'

The next line, which ends the chapter, caught my attention.

'And with all this new data,' he writes, 'we can finally see through people's lies.'

I'm not immune to the excitement of Big Data.

We use data to understand who our customers are and what they're looking for.

We use data to understand where best to locate servers for speed. To ensure that we can guarantee uptime. We use data to understand which type of imagery performs best (as in how many more people click on an image of Madame Gandhi versus Gandhi).

And increasingly we use it to understand how we can offer more creative solutions to our customers.

There is a Japanese philosophy (of course) called Omotenashi. It focuses on human-to-human interaction. The basic principles are as follows.

1. The anticipation of the other's needs. The host should respond to a guest's needs before the latter feels such need himself.
2. Flexibility to the situation. Refers to the appropriate amount of formality or casualness respectively.
3. Understatement. The host should not display his efforts, in order to create a natural feeling for the guest.

It's not that we don't have access to data, it's that we choose to use it responsibly. It's the same as a trustworthy bank. Sure, they have access to all of your money, but do they choose to leverage it all?

The love of Big Data was starting to sound like something else, something larger and larger, and gleefully out of control. I'm not the only one to notice the omnivorous appetite of Big Data extraction systems – in love with their own ability to consume, able to eat up whatever they want, indiscriminate, fat and getting fatter, never satisfied.

As it gets bigger and bigger, Big Data will reportedly tell us more truths. For some, the data reveals us in new ways. For others, such as John Cheney-Lippold, a professor of American Culture and Digital Studies at the University of Michigan, Big Data doesn't speak our hidden truths. Instead, it actually speaks *for* us.

Big Data won't eradicate lying. It's just that the definition of 'lying' changes. We're flooded with 'truths'. Algorithms, Cheney-Lippold explains in his book *We Are Data*, can do anything. They can effectively ventriloquize our data. If you wanted to, algorithms could 'make our data speak as if we were a man, woman, Santa Claus, citizen, Asian, and/or wealthy'.

These would all be true. This data builds 'a proprietary vocabulary that speaks *for* us – to marketers, political campaigns, government dragnets, and others – whether we know about it, like it, or not. Who we are in the face of algorithmic interpretation is who we are calculated to be.'

He continues: 'When our embodied individualities get ignored, we increasingly lose control not just over life but over how life itself is defined.'

Big Data evangelicals speak of honesty, truthfulness, unguarded data that reflects the world as it truly is. Cheney-Lippold brings more nuance. Our online selves are not just endless oil derricks of truth. Which self do they want? We've got a few they can choose from.

For him, this online self 'to borrow the overused phraseology of pop psychology, is a schizophrenic phenomenon. We are likely made a thousand times over in the course of just one day.'

Disclosure to one rectangular box might offer some interesting stats but the voraciousness of the Big Data project brings about a more complicated reality.

'Who we are,' Cheney-Lippold writes, 'is composed of an almost innumerable collection of interpretive layers, of hundreds of different companies and agencies identifying us in thousands of competing ways. At this very moment Google may algorithmically think I'm male, whereas digital advertising company Quantcast could say I'm female, and web-analytic firm Alexa might be unsure. Who is right? Well, nobody really.'

What's being constructed is a secondary text that we don't ever get a chance to read. 'We have reached the point,' writes Shoshana Zuboff in her opus *The Age of Surveillance Capitalism*, 'at which there is little that is omitted from the continuous accretion of this new electronic text ... [which] spreads silently but relentlessly, like a colossal oil slick engulfing everything in its path.'

Who gets to make sense of Big Data? 'The essential questions,' Zuboff writes, 'confront us at every turn: *Who knows? Who decides? Who decides who decides?*'

Before I get to why it might be good business, let's just look at what incessant data mining does to the infrastructure of our online world. How might the cracks form? You're never going to get a venture capitalist to listen to the following (not many), not yet, but hey, the thought is out there. Can we trust it? Can we as business people ask some big questions? Will data mining stop us from developing as businesses? As people?

(Sorry to bring the notion of a catastrophic hindrance of the development of self to your airport reading but, hey, here it is.)

'When identity is formed without our conscious interaction with others, we are never free to develop – nor do we know how to develop,' Cheney-Lippold writes. Google might look at your search terms and assume a gender. Is that a big deal? 'What an algorithmic gender signifies is something largely illegible to us, although it remains increasingly efficacious for those who are using our data to market, surveil, or control us.'

Political economist Oscar Gandy points out: 'The use of predictive models based on historical data is inherently conservative.'

With this chorus of criticism, will there be a time when Big Data starts to look like a public health concern? Who knows? Should our kids be under surveillance, defined and stuck in proprietary categories from birth onwards?

Or would you prefer a childhood that is somehow more organic?

Here's Cheney-Lippold again: 'In an online world of endlessly overhauled algorithmic knowledge, Google's misrepresentation of my gender and age isn't an error. It's a reconfiguration, a freshly minted algorithmic truth that cares little about being authentic but cares a lot about being an effective metric for classification.'

Let's rein it back a bit. This is, after all, supposed to be a book about making a billion dollars by not pestering your users online. Some say Big Data will reveal who we are (even if we're lying to our IRL friends). Some say it will tell us, forcefully, unendingly, exactly who we are.

What lurks in the background is another question.

Will people someday get sick enough of both inadvertently exposing their truths and secretly having roles and traits assigned to them?

The 'right to be forgotten' sounds a little like a Milan Kundera novel – before it became policy. Maybe the sequel will be the 'right to control how life is defined'?

Increasingly, people turn to us when they intuit there could be a business opportunity here. Is there money to be made? In a way, the problems we're seeing with Big Data and its seemingly inevitable importance in our lives reveal a vulnerability. We all may draw the line somewhere.

I'm reminded of a Deloitte study quoted in Zuboff's book. The subject was auto insurance and the increased monitoring of drivers using telemetry – the process of recording and transmitting information. Deloitte acknowledged that 'according to its own survey data, most consumers reject telematics on the basis of privacy concerns and mistrust companies that want to monitor their behavior. This reluctance can be overcome, the consultants advise, by offering cost savings "significant enough" that people are willing "to make the [privacy] trade-off," in spite of "lingering concerns."'

What if those concerns continue to linger for those confronted with Big Data in all its forms? That's a big what if.

But the tech world is not immune from people finding out how they're being used.

Although we valued the data we collected from our users, at WeTransfer we started to realize we were now on the other side of what seems to be the most important divide of our time. Perhaps this process started as just an incomplete and naive understanding of the future of the internet. Perhaps it was because we viewed the world in too simple a manner. Perhaps it was luck.

Back in 2009, we set up a service that trimmed the amount of data we asked for. We had no sign-up. We didn't ask people to create an account. This might not seem like a big deal.

But this is the single move that became one of the most compelling and groundbreaking aspects of WeTransfer and still sets us apart from the data extractors. It was, some would unfortunately say, our game changer. (I'm never going to use that phrase again.) For better or worse, we were distinguished from the rest. This became the USP that sets us apart from the competition. It became the calling card that separates WeTransfer from nearly every other tech business out there.

If the little rectangular box of a Google search defines its ambitions to collect and compile, our sign-up box hinted at our own burgeoning beliefs:

Leave people alone.

This meant that the amount of data we would collect on and about our users would be very limited. Compound this with an advertising format that couldn't be sold by the programmatic websites of the world, and we were left with nearly zero data.

Between the years of 2009 and 2015, this was seen by advertisers, and sales houses and brands, investors and corporations as a serious shortcoming. Like: What the hell are you doing? Like: Why not reach out and grab what's in front of you? Like: Are you guys high on Dutch weed? Look at all the cash you're leaving on the table.

It was, at best, a missed opportunity. At worst, we were dismissed as tech guys who unfortunately just didn't understand tech. Which would seem to be a crucial thing to understand.

There was, of course, some degree of truth in this. I can admit that now. None of us were hugely tech literate. None of us came from an engineering school or university where we had learned to code C++, Python, Ruby or any other language. But we had stuff going for us. We could speak multiple languages. We understood the language of design and the experience of design. We firmly understood that our attitude towards sign-up could be a disruption. Maybe not the kind of disruption people were used to. 'Disruption-by-trusting-our-users' wasn't exactly a buzzword or a TED Talk. We could, we realized, disrupt an environment where people were asked to hand over information before they'd received anything in return. This disruption stemmed from a truly crazy, mind-bending concept: actual loyalty.

Perhaps it was our archaic, European view of the world. Perhaps this was our Dutchness shining through again. We couldn't shake the fact we didn't need to ditch our own values when we went online. We couldn't recall ever visiting a physical store in the real world that would ask us to sign up for a loyalty card prior to having purchased anything. We were going to apply the same utterly loony bit of disruptive thinking to the online world. If a store in the real world didn't ask you, why would any internet business ask you?

As the behemoth that is data extraction charges forward, this choice feels like more of a disruption, year after year. Back then, we were helped by our size. We were a tiny team with no money. The more complex we made the product, the more people we needed, and the greater the cost.

In 2010 we had just enough money to pay a small legal team to advise us. I spent a big chunk of my time working behind the scenes, ensuring our terms and conditions and privacy policy were simple. Lean – as we liked to call it. I spent a lot of time ensuring that, unlike any other business of our ilk, we had dead simple legal speak. Our terms were easy to understand, even our employment contracts. Everything should be set up in a way that was inclusive and obvious. It wasn't difficult to set ourselves apart from the rest of the file sharing crowd.

File sharing in 2009–2010 was dominated by businesses that were mostly interested in piracy and porn. We wanted to ensure that we weren't. We held our head high and stayed clear of the pirates. I joined the Notice and Take Down Policy Group in 2010, to ensure we were actively involved in bodies that were out to protect copyright, prevent piracy and deter misuse on the platform.

All the while our lean data policy was supported by one

of the best customer support teams in the world, constantly helping to keep users happy, being on call 24/7 and escalating issues when necessary. Shout-out to customer support! They're game changers! (I know, I said I'd never use that phrase again.)

There was more evidence of our wild appetite to disrupt: you didn't need to share the details of your life with us to get customer service. As we all know, the internet can be a dark place. We started to notice that where there were huge amounts of security, encryption and firewalls, the internet's underworld found refuge. When there was transparency and trust, the underworld tended to flee.

Knock on wood.

In the meantime, our simple service has transferred over 100 billion files to every corner of the globe. We've noticed the majority of our users are professional and grateful that we provide a mostly faultless, simple service.

Sometimes – like anyone involved in tech – I think about what we could possibly learn from them, what details we could take from them, how interesting it might be to monitor and dissect and scrutinize their moves, their content, their choices. Of course that urge is there. I can understand Stephens-Davidowitz's enamoured view of Big Data as 'digital truth serum'.

But Big Data is not a practice or a disruptive tool. It's an environment. It's being used to aid a new, rampaging form of capitalism – voracious and looking to suction up endless amounts of our data. That's not hyperbole at this point.

Some companies will go in with everything they've got.

We're already seeing toy companies and insurance companies enraptured by the idea of capturing data. It begins to resemble full-bore mining. Some, without expertise, will get mired down in the world of Big Data, awash in numbers with no real way of discerning what they mean.

For various different reasons, more and more will go lean. There will be a movement towards responsible tech.

For inspiration, we've always looked towards some of the aforementioned real-world companies. Being responsible doesn't mean getting abused or going belly-up. Look at REI Co-op, the place to go for outdoor clothing and gear. How is it that a business as successful and loved as REI can offer an unlimited, no questions asked, full refund, full return policy and not get abused?

The choice is whether you want to live in a world where you expect the worst from people, or one where you expect the best?

I don't want to make it sound like it's easy to find allies. Our business development team spends a large chunk of its time seeking out potential partners. They look for companies who might embark on collaborations with us, companies that might share our values and beliefs. During one session, we drew a chart listing all the tech companies that we felt aligned with us.

Two minutes later we took a break.

In the for-profit world the list consisted of: Lyft, Firefox, Omidyar Network, DuckDuckGo, Craigslist and Aspiration bank. There was an incredibly long list of companies that didn't fit with our values. I'm sure you can guess a few names.

In the not-for-profit world the task was a lot easier. If we considered retail we would include the following companies: Patagonia, REI (as mentioned already), Ben & Jerry's, TOMS Shoes, SpiderOak.

What was evident was that there was not a single advertising business on the internet doing what we do. There was not a single SaaS business on the internet doing what we do. There were very few venture-backed businesses doing what we do.

Still, it feels like the right direction.

(Fingers crossed.)

Let's look more closely at one success story. The search engine DuckDuckGo has had a very clear mission from the beginning: 'Too many people believe that you simply can't expect privacy on the Internet. We disagree and have made it our mission to set a new standard of trust online.'

DDG pops up all the time on those 'How to Protect Your Digital Life in 9 Easy Steps' lists. It always gets mentioned when there's yet another Facebook break-in. It seems that in the last few years the message is getting through to people who have been burned one too many times. DDG are not interested in shrouding their beliefs in highfalutin ideals or impenetrable tech-speak.

'At DuckDuckGo,' their website states, 'we don't think the Internet should feel so creepy and getting the privacy you deserve online should be as simple as closing the blinds.'

Privacy should be the default. The company knows, as do we, that users need to be led back. They need to be reminded of what has been so swiftly taken away.

We're living through a time where people could easily forget the importance of privacy. And instead of castigating the world, like some angry screeching preacher on a mountaintop, there are ways to lead people back.

At its core DDG is a search engine, but they also understand the need to take on the identity of a teacher – a pleasant teacher – with blog posts that seem to be written by their mascot, a talking duck named Dax.

Just recently, DuckDuckGo released on their blog an article schooling their users. It was called 'Three Reasons Why the "Nothing to Hide" Argument Is Flawed' and tucked away in the answers were sentiments that would have seemed obvious a few years ago.

'Simply put,' read the last line in one reason, 'everyone wants to keep certain things private and you can easily illustrate that by asking people to let you make all their emails, texts, searches, financial information, medical information, etc. public. Very few people will say yes.'

All this benevolent teaching is fine and good, but DDG have, since the beginning, also held the belief that this approach can work, can make money, and will only become more popular as we're dredged for more and more data. They've been around since 2008 and have, from the outset, been interested in demonstrating there could be money made, eventually, by those who don't trample users' privacy needs.

Back in January 2018 they expanded the mobile app and the necessary browser extension. According to their website, they're up to 21 billion searches.

The answer, for DDG, comes from advertising. Again, like

us, they employ a throwback model. 'If you type in "car" you get a car ad, if you type in "mortgage" you get a mortgage ad,' its founder Gabriel Weinberg told *Wired*. 'We don't need to know about you or your search history to deliver a lucrative ad.'

There something confident about the 'we don't need to know about you' in the statement above. Perhaps this is the beginning of companies simplifying the relationship, reconsidering what is necessary. For DDG, the transaction is just fine without access to a search history. There's trust involved.

I mean, you're still going to see an ad. There's no way of getting around that.

It benefits DDG to remind people about the severity of the recent scandals. It benefits us to get people to feel this sort of thing as they might feel pain on their skin. There are many in the tech world who would like to underplay the importance of what's erupted in the last year. The Cambridge Analytica scandal was, according to Facebook, pretty bad. 'People's privacy and security is incredibly important, and we're sorry this happened,' Facebook said when the scandal erupted. Because they are the only game in town, Facebook is able to perform, again and again, a meaningless ritual of contrition. 'Because Facebook so dominates social networking,' co-founder Chris Hughes wrote, in May 2019, 'it faces no market-based accountability. This means that every time Facebook messes up, we repeat an exhausting pattern: first outrage, then disappointment and, finally, resignation.'

In September, 2018, they announced at least 50 million and

potentially up to 90 million Facebook users had their data exposed to hackers. Fifty million? That's like all of Kenya getting hacked. It benefits companies like DDG and our own to remind users – even employing the skills of an animated talking duck – that this stuff is seriously worthy of more than another 'sorry'.

The Big Data titans would like us to follow them into the reality of the new normal, where it's normal to give up everything, no matter how many times we get abused. The new normal is acquiescence. It's difficult to get some people to forget the old normal: that the responsibility of holding data is serious.

The issues that have arisen through the General Data Protection Regulation (GDPR) go to the core of how we want to live. The aftermath of Cambridge Analytica has rippled through Silicon Valley and, hopefully, into the lives of those who use their products. I'm confident to say this is just the beginning.

We'll see many more companies follow down the path of responsible data. We'll pay these companies for their services. We'll make some people very rich. (The data extractors will inevitably get richer, but still . . .)

Instead of summing up their words, I decided to speak to a few of our allies on the web.

Gabriel Weinberg is CEO of DuckDuckGo, and after learning many interesting things about privacy from their talking duck, I decided I should speak to a real person. Why not start at the top? Weinberg started his bare-bones search engine at home in Pennsylvania. He was complimented by all sorts of sources. The site was compared by *Time* magazine to hamburger restaurant In-N-Out. 'Just as In-N-Out doesn't have lattes or Asian salads or sundaes or scrambled eggs, DDG doesn't try to do news or blogs or books or images.'

Weinberg was able to grow slowly away from the In-N-Out comparisons. DDG now offers news and blogs and images in the search engine and considers itself an internet privacy company, not just a search engine, with tracker blocking and smarter encryption along with private search.

DuckDuckGo:
A Conversation with Gabriel Weinberg

Gabriel: I had another company which I sold. Then I was looking for something to do more long term. But really I wasn't sure what that was, and so I tried to ideate.

Then I realized I was not going to be doing a good job with that.

So, like WeTransfer, I started a bunch of side projects, and tried to see what stuck in terms of my interests. A lot of those ended up being search related: trying to get SEO, building something to remove bad clicks.

The other piece was instant answers, similar to Wikipedia. There were sets of links out there. For instance, Wikipedia external links were often better than Google's top results for certain things.

So I decided all of those things could then be put together maybe, to make an interesting search experience.

I started playing around with that as a product. My job

from 2007 to 2010 was just a lot of iteration. I had a first child at the time. I was a stay-at-home dad, so I was just doing it on the side, and responding to feedback and trying to make it better.

In that time period, shortly after launching and listening to the feedback, I had more questions and did a few deeper investigations on privacy and search privacy.

I have a graduate degree in technology policy, so these internet policy issues interested me. It piqued my interest when people were asking about the privacy policy.

Here's one example. In 2006, AOL released a data set of search queries that was supposedly anonymous, but they were tied together via a unique identifier and people were able to de-anonymize a bunch of people in it.

In 2009, Netflix had this Netflix Prize where they also put out a data set that they claimed was anonymous, but it had session data and people were able to de-anonymize the data.

And then there were some high-profile cases, Yahoo among them. It was not exactly search related – that was more email – but it was about storing information on people and then handing that data over to China. The person responsible was jailed, culminating in a hearing where Yahoo went up in front of the US Congress.

This investigation made me realize a couple of things.

One was that private information could have real-world consequences to people like dissidents.

Ten years ago, policy people were thinking about things that are starting to come true now.

What if health insurers got access to your searches and could charge you different prices? What if retailers knew your search history and could charge you different prices? Both of those things are happening now. What if governments across the world, not just China, were starting to use this information against you? I realized that it could be harmful to people.

The second revelation was, it wasn't necessary to track searches in order to deliver good search results or ads. The business itself is uniquely positioned to not store any information because you type in your intent and you can give ads based on that intent. The search results generally are based solely on the keywords you type, and you can still derive signals anonymously. Just see in aggregate what people click on, nothing to do with the user session.

And then the third thing I realized was that any kind of user session can be de-anonymized. There's no such thing as anonymous session data, as far as I'm concerned. As soon as you have so-called anonymous session data, you can find something to pair it with that de-anonymizes it.

So if you take all those things together, it seemed like you could run a search engine that would be a better user experience for the user.

So I made that decision in 2009.

In early 2010, I publicly announced that's what we did.

But at that point, it wasn't that much of a motivator in terms of attracting people to the site. It was still pretty much an edge concept, because the harms were not very well known.

There was interest in a small sub-set of the community, but we were still attracting people more for those other reasons, like instant answers, customization, less spam.

All of those dwarfed the privacy reason for a while.

Damian: And then you launched as DuckDuckGo?

Gabriel: Then we launched as DuckDuckGo.

Over time, it became clear that there were very few things that allow you to compete against Google. It has to be something that they can't copy technically, which is easy for them. A lot of the features that we had originally used to differentiate ourselves were eventually copied – spam and instant answers.

It has to be for another reason, a legal, business reason. So one of the remaining things that differentiated us was privacy. For structural reasons, they have gone – and continue to go – in a completely 'get as much data as you can' direction.

And as they march in that direction, our differentiation becomes more clear. And as the world has gone in that direction, it becomes more needed.

So then, in 2013 is when the real step function happened, with the NSA revelations and the recognition that actually some of the things we were talking about and the reason why we don't track were true.

There was this backdoor gateway to searches in Google, in particular, that the government has, and so that was the one sticking point for government surveillance.

Since 2013, the corporate surveillance side has increased, increased and increased.

That had its big sticking point in 2018 with Cambridge Analytica.

We were seeing it way before, though. Even back in 2012, Google changed their privacy policy to allow sharing data between its services, which is now why people are up in arms – correctly – about Facebook.

Google were anticipating that earlier because they had bought DoubleClick and then started finding these things; they wanted to store data, and then over time, almost every year there's been a walking back of any kind of Chinese wall between different things in their privacy policy.

The last one was, I think, in 2016, where they finally said, basically: 'We're building a big profile of you and we're using it across all of our advertising networks the same way.'

Your searches will follow you around. That has happened more and more, along with various harms like the filter bubble and manipulations through ads. All those different things have become more and more harmful. We stand as an alternative.

Damian: Do people give a shit? On Amazon, the convenience of getting a Swiffer mop within two hours is a killer. Convenience wins, right?

Gabriel: Yeah.

Damian: This was really the most interesting revelation for me: convenience is such a drug that people seem to talk a good game when it comes to privacy, but I didn't see that many people do anything about it. Your numbers would suggest otherwise.

Gabriel: There are a couple of ways to look at this. We're more than just a search engine, but let's discuss search for just a second.

Let's say we were literally exactly the same – to the extent that there was no sacrifice whatsoever in switching, even in terms of design. Then it becomes a no-brainer. I think people really do want more privacy if they can get it for free. Right?

And so, the closer you get to that line of 'you're just as convenient, you're just as good, potentially even better in some cases' then the more people switch.

Because people do care. They do want privacy. The question is how much do they want it? How much are they willing to give up in different situations?

We found as our product gets better and better, and it's easier and easier to switch, then we have more adoption.

Then there is the second question. For different people, in different places, there are all sorts of different privacy harms. They care about privacy to different degrees. People are willing to go different amounts of sacrifice. And so we find that as the awareness of the harms increase, people are willing to do a bit more, right?

That's what we've seen over the past few years. The harms have increased. There are more and more creepy ads. There are more and more data breaches. There's more and more identity theft.

Those three things drive a lot of interest.

People are seeing those harms a lot more. And it's been easier to switch. So you see adoption grow as a result.

There's another piece. We realize privacy is really complicated for people to understand because it's a really complicated concept. There are all these different harms, all these technologies you have to use to help yourself.

We see our role as simplifying – both in terms of education but also in delivering the one tool that can help you reduce your footprint online. And so our latest iteration of our apps and extensions have all the privacy essentials in them that you need.

You use it to search, but it's also tracker blocking, encryption, all in one package. And what we can say to people is: 'It's available on every browser and device. All you have to do is find DuckDuckGo, and you've kind of done the 80/20, and you're in this more safe environment.'

So, from people's perspective, there's this big bad

internet where all these companies are trying to exploit them, and if you adopt DuckDuckGo, you're not having all those sacrifices, just changing your browser and search engine, and it's a nice, safer world. That trade-off is easier to make.

That said, I think if the sacrifice was really great, then I think you'd be right. If we were charging people ten bucks a month, we would have a lot less users.

Or, if you couldn't get any search results. If it was really, really worse, then it wouldn't work either.

Damian: Do you have profiles of your users?

Gabriel: So this is quite interesting. We have a blog, it's spreadprivacy.com.

There's the research side of it where we've continually done mainstream research, surveys on privacy, trying to figure out our target market: who says they're concerned. But beyond that, who actually acts on it. Who's actually adopting DuckDuckGo or other privacy tools?

The interesting part is that it cuts across all demographics. There's no signal in that, in normal demographic terms. It cuts across political parties, ages, income, education. We're finding essentially representative groups of all.

Damian: And country specific?

Gabriel: To a degree. North America, Europe and Australia, New Zealand – we have generally similar market share adoption. It's not like there's a huge spike in Europe versus the US or anywhere else.

Damian: Where are your servers or who's hosting them?

Gabriel: AWS. We now are in five different regions but we can be in more. We just haven't done it.

Damian: And you don't have any concerns in having your data hosted on Amazon Web Services?

Gabriel: So we've constructed it so that we are in control of all the servers, and we basically don't use any of their tools that involve handling encryption keys.

This is a nuanced topic, but I think it's actually more secure than hosting on a random hosting platform.

You have to host somewhere, right? And so if you're in a random hardware that isn't yours there's a whole bunch of other physical security concerns that one has that are harder to control for than, I think, in the virtual server environment.

In any case, the short answer is we encrypt everything to our boxes and only we see it. We also don't log anything in terms of personal information. So it's only sending on the wire to us encrypted and then sending back encrypted and then we don't store anything.

Damian: When I've explained DuckDuckGo, I've struggled even to explain how something like DuckDuckGo can serve up Google search and it not be part of Google. Could you explain for my mum? How is it safer or simpler to use you guys than it is to just use Chrome?

Gabriel: There are multiple ways to adopt us. You can use Chrome and install the DuckDuckGo browser extension.

What that will do is twofold. When you surf around the web, Google is tracking you everywhere you go, pretty much. They're on like 75 per cent of websites, lurking in the background.

What our extension does is blocks their trackers across the web – as well as Facebook's and all sorts of other data brokers, bad actors.

When you search, there are more search engines than Google. So they can be delivered by somebody else. We provide a private search engine so that when you do a search, we can serve results to you anonymously. So when you search DuckDuckGo it's like you've never been there before. Whereas Google saves all your search history and then uses that to target ads to you across the web.

When you use DuckDuckGo your search is anonymous. Then when you click on those sites we block Google, as well as trackers.

Then when you click on those sites we also block Google on those sites.

So you're experiencing the web, kind of Google free, essentially.

The most practical effect is that you immediately stop

seeing those ads that follow you around everywhere. That's a sign that people aren't following you any more.

Damian: But couldn't you just use private browsing mode on Chrome? Isn't it the same?

Gabriel: It is not the same. That is a big myth that I would love to dispel.

Private browsing mode: all it does is scrub the data from your computer when you're done with private browsing mode.

It does not prevent anyone on the other side of the connection from tracking you. And so when you go to a website in private browsing mode, that website can still see your computer IP address and everything about your computer. They can associate that with a profile on their side. So even though your history's deleted on your side, they still have it on their side.

So Google can still be tracking across the web even in private browsing.

Damian: So how do we educate people more?

What experience have you had in educating people that works?

Gabriel: I'd say two broad areas.

We use the blog as a platform to kind of get wider mainstream press on the issues. So we've been doing original research or original commentary that then gets picked up and so I think that has worked pretty well.

We've been writing long-form Quora answers and other blog posts.

They really go in depth and explain these things. We've been advertising those to get people on them at points of interest. That's actually worked a lot.

It's a good selling point. With WeTransfer, my sense, just looking at it, is you could do more in that messaging inside the product, somehow, to educate.

What we found is, we spend a lot of time writing these long-form things in a really mainstream, readable way.

In your case, to the audience of creatives, one day each creative will be in the moment of wanting to read this thing. Then they'll finally read it and you'll slowly be educating them, over time.

It won't magically work the first day you put it up. But it has worked, over time.

For example, on the DuckDuckGo footer, you just search and you look at the bottom. We have these cards. Some small percentage of people click every day, but over a long period of time, say the next two years, our assessment is that most will eventually click on it. You know? And then they'll maybe read it.

Damian: Are you optimistic about the future? Do you think that we're going to get to a place where people are much more educated around privacy?

Gabriel: I think so. I'm pretty optimistic about it after last year.

Damian: What about Google? Where are they gonna go? What's gonna happen to them and Facebook?

Gabriel: I'm not optimistic that they're going to implode or change their practices very much, but I'm optimistic that people are getting awareness, making different choices.

That is translating into some kind of privacy legislation in different places worldwide, including the US, where people basically laughed at you if you mentioned it a year ago. You know?

So that has drastically changed. That's a good environment to be optimistic about. And generally, what you find here is that it all follows from the will of the people.

People say: 'Oh that'll never happen.' But as soon as you start getting polling numbers, people start voting on an issue, everything can change quickly.

That started happening on privacy – at least, that's the test this year. If nothing really happens after this year then I might be more pessimistic next year.

•••

In any book about trust, it's important to speak to those working in industries considered untrustworthy. Andrei Cherny is the CEO and co-founder of Aspiration.com, a rare bright spot in the banking world. Much like the real-estate industry, banking is dogged with a legacy of corruption, overcharging, contempt for customers and unfairness. For many, the day Lehman

Brothers closed down is now the distant past. But the financial industry doesn't seem to have learned anything in the years that have passed. Banks have once again started trading credit default swaps. Student loan defaults have increased. The industry has found inevitable loopholes to escape the consequences. Where there is money, big money, there will always be a way.

A bank that treats its customers fairly is hard to find. A bank that gives back to its community is a nice notion and probably exists alongside Sasquatches in some alternative dimension. We can make jokes. We can grumble, but it's important to remind ourselves of the bitter truth. We need the banking industry. But we need more banks and financial institutions that behave like Aspiration. Ultimately, it's these lenders who will set the goals and levels of ambition for business – in particular tech business. And today, every business is a tech business.

Unsurprisingly, the issue of trust came up right away with Andrei. It seems to dictate much of what they do.

On Trust in the Least Trusted Industry
A Conversation with Andrei Cherny

Andrei: Internally, when we're having a meeting, a discussion, and just wrestling with a problem, our motto is 'solve for trust'. When you're looking at banking and the financial industry, you're looking at an industry where 8 per cent of Americans say they trust their financial institution. And it always seems to me that if you're not first and foremost solving for that problem, you're missing the 800-pound gorilla in the room.

It's great to have lower fees, and better technology, and cool features. All of those things are necessary, but they're not speaking to the central core challenge that people have, especially when it comes to the financial industry.

The banking experience used to be a community experience, a local experience.

There was the experience of having a person that you knew, who you saw at your kids' Little League game or supermarket.

Then there was a wave of conglomeration. That local experience has now disappeared. And so there's a space for using technology, not to replace human interaction, but to scale human interaction.

You had a financial industry that made a pivot in how it made money – to really focus on fees as the main driver of interaction, and fees around financial illness as opposed to financial health.

The big banks make money when things go wrong for you. When you have an overdraft fee, when you have a late fee, an out-of-network ATM fee, when you have monthly service fees because you don't have enough deposits in your account, and so on.

That means there's a fundamental misalignment of interests between people and their financial institution.

We wanted to solve for that, and we also understood that there's a misalignment of values. People's expectations of the places they're doing business with, in this day and age, have changed. They're looking to those businesses to have a conscience and a sense of ethics and values. And that certainly wasn't the case in the financial industry.

Damian: I'm trying to find companies that are ethically minded, or values driven, or have strongly ingrained CSR [corporate social responsibility] approach within the business. It's exceptionally hard to find it within anything other than retail: Patagonia, TOMS, Ben & Jerry's, those guys have been doing it for between ten and twenty years. We're a Dutch company, so banks like Triodos have been around quite a while, and are quite well known in the Netherlands, but not well known really outside of it.

But in the tech and the finance world, there are very few companies that have built into their DNA an ethical approach to business. I can barely think of any.

Andrei: For us, the two were always linked.

Previously, I had just spent a number of years in the public policy space and worked in the White House and the Clinton administration, and worked with Elizabeth Warren on the idea for what became the Consumer Financial Protection Bureau. I was a financial fraud prosecutor, and so on, doing consulting, and some of it for big banks and large institutions. I saw these very large institutions who were trying to bolt on a corporate social responsibility program.

People saw right through that.

We said we didn't want to be a business that was making money in ways that were fundamentally at odds with the best interests and values of our consumers – and then do some nice things on the side. We wanted those two to be inextricably linked. We would only make money to the extent that we were doing the right thing in the right way for our customers.

This led to the 'pay what is fair' fee structure, where we said we were going to let the customer choose the fee.

It's not a free service by any means. There is a fee. As opposed to us setting the fee, we want the customer to pick the fee, and if they think we deserve to be paid zero, then we deserve to be paid zero, and we need to be doing a better job. But then it's up to us to deliver for that customer – whether it's in the service we provide, or the values – in such a way that they choose to pay us even though they don't have to.

We were going to believe that our customers were going to treat us with the same kind of honesty and integrity that they're expecting us to show them.

That seemed natural. We really wanted to do things differently and build a strong charitable commitment into it as well.

It's been three years now.

Damian: Can you demonstrate that it's working?

Andrei: Which part? The business?

Damian: Here's what we're competing with: a huge chunk of the tech industry is very financially driven, so a lot of the employees are simply going for the highest salary, the best perks, and the best options package, which leads to a phenomenal amount of churn.

I'm not going to compete with Google and Snapchat and everybody else, because I don't believe in competing on purely financial terms.

What we're offering is a different mindset. But I haven't yet found a way of putting it into any sort of numerical system that actually can justify how it's working. Have you managed to achieve something like that?

Andrei: We see this working in terms of customer growth. We're nearly at two million users at this point, and growing very rapidly. We see it in our ring of social media engagement.

You see the vast majority of customers choosing to pay, even though they don't have to.

That really speaks to the depth of that relationship we've been able to forge. We now have over a hundred employees. We've always insisted that we only hire people who are very mission driven.

I don't have a numerical value I can assign, but I certainly feel what we're going to offer our employees is something different.

If you come into our offices we have IKEA furniture for our commons table. There isn't art on the wall. We don't have free lunches for employees, or other perks like that.

But we also make sure our customers never have to pay an ATM fee, and we give 10 per cent of everything we make towards charitable giving. And we say to our employees, if you like those other things there's absolutely nothing wrong with that. There are plenty of other companies you can go work at.

We provide something different, and we've built a team and a culture around that.

Damian: Who selects the charities? Do you have a CSR department or is everybody involved?

Andrei: People are involved in different ways. What we've at least been historically doing is working primarily with a single charity, which is Accion, around charitable micro loans.

Accion USA network is the largest charitable provider of micro loans in the United States. So they're giving loans to low-income individuals who are looking to make a change in their life, and so that's been our charitable partner and they'll tell us stories around that.

Damian: You've either been really lucky with your investors or you've chosen them very strategically. Not every investor would be interested in a business like yours, right?

Andrei: We have been lucky. We've chosen strategically and, to be honest, we've had an endless number of doors close in our face as well, along the way.

Damian: I'm glad to hear that it wasn't just me.

Andrei: Look, we started a business – my co-founder and I – saying we were going to be a financial business focused on everyday people and not the very wealthy. We were going to let people pay us whatever they want, including zero. We were going to give 10 per cent of what we earn towards charitable giving. As you can imagine, there were initially some very short conversations.

It's interesting. The first major investor who really believed in us was Jeff Skoll, who was president of eBay, and created the Skoll Foundation. I remember sitting down with him and describing what we were doing, and he said: 'Guys, I think this is going to work.'

I said: 'Well, maybe you didn't hear me. Here's what we're doing.' And he said: 'Nah, nah. I think it's going to work.'

This speaks directly to what you're talking about. He said: 'Every ten years or so there is a company or companies that come along that make a big bet on trust.' He said that is what made eBay successful, twenty-plus years ago.

In the early days of the internet, it was the Wild West, and all of their competitors had these complicated escrow models.

You're just going to have to believe that this person you've never met before, that you've paid money to over the internet, is actually going to send you that baseball card, or whatever else it is. And similarly, if you said ten years ago that there would be big businesses based on getting into a stranger's car, or staying in a stranger's bedroom in a foreign country, you know, people would have said that's crazy. And certainly you've had the Airbnbs, Ubers, Lyfts, and so on, that have come along. And he said similarly, you're taking this big bet on trust. It's going to pay off for you.

● ● ●

I wanted to take a break from the story of my company to ask Jimmy Wales, co-founder of Wikipedia, what we're going to do. By that I mean the greater 'us', the general public. What are we going to do about the internet of the future, because, as I told him, I fundamentally believe it's down to you and me, as in 'those people in the street'. I've discussed what a responsible tech company like mine could do. It's not down to business people to shape what the internet looks like. The user has this idea that they have no control over what's happening. I truly believe the reverse is true. All the power is in the hands of the user. They just feel powerless.

Some people who have been very much involved with the internet from the very beginning, or from the early days, are still absolutely 100 per cent smitten with what the internet can do and completely unperturbed by Big Data and the potential consequences for the future. And there are those who are absolutely paranoid and living in fear every day, because their five-star rating is basically a make or break for them to receive the next job offer.

I wanted to talk to Jimmy about how he built trust and what – obviously – the future is going to look like.

On Luck and the Benefits of Not Being Given Money
A Conversation with Jimmy Wales

Damian: How old is Wikipedia?

Jimmy: Wikipedia is now seventeen.

It's funny because I never really think in these terms about Wikipedia. I never think of a market for Wikipedia. It's just not the way we ever approached it, which is interesting, I think, in and of itself. In a sense, we are an alcove of early internet culture. But I don't think that meant that we thought that Wikipedia was only for hobbyists because already, by the time Wikipedia started in 2001, the internet was already quite big.

We had already been through most of the dotcom boom, and Google existed. Facebook didn't yet, but lots of things that we know about were already familiar and existing. I didn't think of it as a hobbyist market, if I thought of it as a market at all.

Internet on your phone was, if at all, very hard to use and basically didn't work, like those pre-smart phones. So it was very much desktop: laptops, and real desktop computers.

In that sense, obviously, it was very different than the environment we look at today. Maybe slightly more than 50 per cent of our traffic is by mobile. So that's different in a lot of ways, including what does it mean to participate at

Wikipedia? Obviously, the vast majority of people who are editing Wikipedia are on a desktop. Editing from a little device is not particularly comfortable. People do it, but it's not easy. Which means that there are loads and loads of readers who probably won't convert very easily to becoming authors, potentially because they're readers on their devices. That's an interesting kind of dynamic that's going on.

Damian: So in and of itself, it's pretty revolutionary that people decided to build something that didn't have a business model behind it.

You haven't, for whatever reason, felt pressured to put one in and do the normal premium service, the pro-version, anything else?

Jimmy: I would think about that in two ways. In the early days, the very early days, it was not unusual, but only because it was the dotcom boom, when I first set up Wikipedia. And at that time, it was really a mentality of 'Don't worry about your business model right now. Just build something.' And so it was pretty common. I mean, obviously, we have some spectacular flame-out failures: services that became quite popular, but literally had no coherent business concept whatsoever. At that time, I remember, Webvan was a famous one that lost, I think, $800 million from doing online delivery of groceries, which, of course, is a growing and big business now, but back then it was just they couldn't make it work. But that was okay. At the moment, they were like, 'Let's just get big, and we'll figure it out.'

And then we had the dotcom crash, and so in many ways, Wikipedia is truly a child of the dotcom crash because, as it began to grow, there was no hope of raising money.

Silicon Valley wasn't investing in anything because everything was a disaster beyond all measure. And that was, in some ways, a blessing for us because a lot of the innovations of Wikipedia came about because we literally had no money. There was no way to solve problems by throwing money at them, which means we had to solve them, but maybe solve them in a more innovative way.

Just a simple thing would be, you would imagine, as a site starts to grow, if we had 10 million, 20 million in capital, we would have said: 'Oh, right. Well, so we're starting to see this problem or that problem. We need to hire community managers and moderators, and pay staff to block people and to enforce the rules and so forth.' And we would have gone right down the model of You-Tube and that sort of thing, where the community actually has no power whatsoever. And the moderators are staff members. And that would've been very, very different, and I think not nearly as successful, nor innovative. But because we didn't have any money, we had to figure it out ourselves – or the community would. We had a lot of the checks and balances that you wouldn't have developed if you had just paid people. You have to sort of say: 'Well, who are the moderators going to be?' It begins to look a lot more like a democracy in the sense of a good municipal government. You need people to enforce the rules, but they have to be accountable. And so the admins, all their actions have to be transparent, and they have to be able to lose their admin rights. And who's going to decide that? And you have to have procedures and processes and things in the community. So we built up all of those things.

How admins are elected by the community, and then how they can lose their admin rights. Things like the arbitration committee, which enforces higher level – kind of like the Supreme Court of Wikipedia. It's a whole set of things that we had to evolve, but they were evolved in light of saying: 'We're just a volunteer community.' And so that also gave us incredible intellectual independence.

Wikipedia from the very early days didn't cost a lot to produce because it wasn't done by staff. It was done by community members.

I decided: 'Okay. Look. We are a non-profit. We need to ask for money. We need to do a fundraiser.' So we did. We announced a fundraiser, and I was hoping to get $20,000 in a month's time, and we had nearly $30,000 within about two weeks' time. So it was a huge success. But that was the first time I really thought: 'Well, just asking people to support Wikipedia might actually be a model that works.' And it has proven to be so.

One of the things a lot of people don't know, although we're super transparent about everything, is if you look at the finances of Wikipedia, it's kinda getting to . . . We'll call it embarrassingly profitable, in the sense that we run the organization in a very financially conservative way. And every year, we spend less than we bring in, and our surpluses have been over 20 million, 15 million. I don't know what it's going to be this year, but we had our best revenue year. We just broke 100 million in revenue. I'm sure we didn't spend even 80.

So as a financial model, it's proven to be surprisingly successful, but it's a charity. So obviously all we do with the money is we just build our reserves for the future and spend it on charitable projects, but it's kind of interesting.

Damian: Is it fair to say that you discovered this by accident?

Jimmy: Yeah. Sort of.

There's a lot of luck involved in anything like this. So of course, there were a hundred decisions a day, every day, not just that I made, but that the community made. It sort of [came about] by accident, but also a lot of trial and error, a lot of hard thinking about the problems and figuring out how to do it. So we didn't know everything a priori, but we had certain conditions a priori, and then we just stuck to those conditions and solved the detail problems as they came up.

Damian: So at any stage, you'd never actually taken any investor capital?

Jimmy: No, zero. Zero. Yeah, Wikipedia is completely self-funded.

Damian: So had you taken investor capital at one moment, it would be a completely different story?

Jimmy: Oh, completely.

Damian: $200,000 from somebody, it would've changed everything?

Jimmy: Totally, totally. Because we would have ended up a for profit, with all the needs that go with that.

Damian: You're a complete anomaly in this because you, as a developer, have taken a very empathetic approach to an online business. You could have changed it massively. This is perhaps not something I'd say publicly, but often, developers are not that empathetic. They're not that community driven. In that sense you are unique.

You could argue that, had Facebook struggled in the way that you struggled, and launched at the same time, Facebook could well be in the same place as Wikipedia today.

Jimmy: It's at least conceivable. Certainly, when we think about the business models of, for example, Facebook, the business models are always the product. Not in every way, but in a lot of ways.

That's kind of interesting to think about something that's so fundamental to society in the social sense, how everyone's using Facebook and sharing photos and things like that. If you think the business model drives the service, and it's Amazon, that's a lot less weird in some way because it's like, yes, Amazon is an e-commerce site that wants to sell you stuff, so the whole business model is about making it easy for you to buy stuff. Make sure the prices are right.

Everything about their business model is consistent with what you'd expect, in an obvious way. Everybody understands it. Whereas with Facebook, there's a lot about their business model that is . . . people are aware . . . the famous line when Mark was speaking to Congress. When he was sort of baffled. 'How do you make money anyways?' He's like: 'We run ads.' Almost everybody except the Senator understands that, but the deeper question is: 'What does that mean in terms of what do they want to drive you to do on the platform? What is the information they want to elicit from you?'

These people are just now beginning to grapple with [the realization that] this model doesn't drive Facebook to make the most wonderful sharing platform, it drives them to get your data. Whereas the business model of Amazon does drive them towards making the most wonderful shopping experience, so it's more aligned.

One of the things that I really talk a lot about with respect to Wikipedia and its business model is the fact that it's a charity. When I say 'this model' in this context, I mean people just donate money because they love Wikipedia and they think it should exist.

If we were a non-profit and we had an advertising business model, then the DNA of the organization would inherently change because organizations do follow the money. That's an inexorable fact. Company culture can resist certain things, but at the end of the day they follow the money.

Right now, the foundation staff care as much about the next million readers in sub-Saharan Africa as they do the next million readers in California because the business model is about being a charity and about making people love us and feel like: 'Wikipedia is the one thing in all these troubling times that I think is basically decent in the world, and I just think I should chip in and support what they're doing.' Which should drive the staff to have a very different set of incentives.

If we were ad focused then I could tell you we would definitely be having an internal meeting looking at revenue. If only people would search more for cheap hotels in Las Vegas rather than Elizabethan poetry, our revenue would jump, so then we'd think about 'let's appease them with clickbait-y headlines and that will get engagement up and da, da, da' and we just don't think in those ways at all. I think it's really interesting to think about how, in some subtle ways, business models drive product in ways that are maybe not always healthy.

Damian: Do you use Facebook personally?

Jimmy: Yeah. I do. I'm a very ordinary consumer of the internet. I use all the usual stuff that everybody uses and I actually like Facebook, so obviously you can see I have great concerns about where their business model drives them. It's a great product. Say what you will about Facebook, it totally works for what most people are trying to use it for. So there is that.

Damian: So you're not concerned?

Jimmy: Sometimes I worry. I worry not in the abstract, I just worry because I'm a non-person on the internet. I'm super careful about all my privacy settings and security, just because I am. In general, I'm like most people. In the last couple of years, the crisis of conscience that happened with the public and the internet companies is kind of the realization that there are side effects. I love programmatic advertising. I love that no matter where I go on the internet, I get ads that are relevant to me. I think that's fantastic. I see a lot of win-win-win in the sense that, if I'm seeing ads that are relevant, that means that the publishers running those ads are going to get paid more because it's not just punch the monkey and all the stupid Tammy ads.

That's great for them, it's great for advertisers because they're partnering with more people. It has the relevance. It's all great. Then you begin to understand: 'On the side, we've got all this weird stuff going on with Cambridge Analytica slicing and dicing for political purposes.'

For me, one of the most disturbing things about that is, in the old days, politicians in order to win had to have a single consistent message, then reach across the middle. That got enough people on board with it. Whereas now it's beginning to feel like they can run campaigns that completely contradict each other. They sell completely different messages to different audiences, and a lot of it's just voter suppression.

That's disturbing, and you realize: 'All that data is out there, and it can be used for more than just making sure that I see boat ads.' That's what I always say, because I like boats. It can be used for all kinds of questionable purposes. That's a dark side effect that I think people are really trying to grapple with.

Damian: You guys are such a beacon of hope for so much about the internet, because there's so much discussion around should the internet be regulated or not? If you look at Wikipedia, Wikipedia has proven that it can actually self-regulate. How does regulation fit in?

Jimmy: I'm no fan of regulation. I'm a First Amendment fan and I'm an entrepreneur and all of that classic stuff. I don't think governments generally do a good job even understanding the internet, much less trying to pass nuanced regulation. So I'm already sceptical. If you're proposing some kind of online regulation that will impact the way people are using the internet, freedom of expression and that sort of thing, you have to say: 'Is this the least intrusive way to achieve a legitimate interest, or are we just splashing around at the behest of the music industry?' or whatever it might be.

There's that. But I'm also very sympathetic. A lot of those problems just don't come up for Wikipedia that do come up for other companies. I just saw there's a big outcry. The other day, Mark Zuckerberg said something along the lines of: 'We won't take down or block people who are engaging in denial of the Holocaust.' People were outraged, because that's really stupid behaviour, people denying the Holocaust, it's hateful – and Mark Zuckerberg is Jewish, even.

But I say: 'You know what? At Wikipedia, we've never allowed Holocaust deniers and we've never allowed loads of things, but also we're not a community free speech platform. We've always said we're here to build an encyclopedia, we're not a platform for people to post all of their opinions. You've gotta have a reliable source. We have an article about Holocaust Denial, but it's quite neutral and, in some ways, would be quite negative because it's historically complete nonsense.

That means we don't have to deal with it. When Twitter struggles with how do you distinguish between legitimate political commentary and saying Donald Trump is an idiot? Or saying Obama's an idiot? Not about Donald Trump. Although he is, in fact, a massive idiot . . . So saying a famous politician is a bad person, insulting them, being rude about them, that's just part of the discourse. That's part of the world, and we don't want to see that kind of thing banned. At the same time, if it's a group of teenagers going in together to bully someone from their class, being insulting and telling lies and getting things wrong and spreading rumours, then we're like: 'Actually, Twitter, why don't you do something about that? It's terrible. Why are you letting this kind of hateful behaviour go on?'

I'm sympathetic. It's a really hard problem for those kinds of platforms. To imagine that politicians can step in and define a magical set of rules that will make the world right is really naive. That really underestimates how complicated that problem is.

When we say, yeah, Wikipedia is a beacon of how you can self-regulate. Yes. Lovely, and I agree. And I think it's a very kind thing to say. But I also would say we've chosen a much easier problem, in a sense. Which is to say, if you go on to Wikipedia and you write *Donald Trump is the worst president in history and I really hate him* and you want to put that into the Wikipedia entry, our community's going to go: 'That's not an encyclopedia, that's just your opinion. Do you have a source?' It's a much easier problem. You deal with hayseeds by going: 'That's not what we do here. We don't care what your opinion is. We're documenting the facts of the world.'

Damian: Your governance is, and has been, strong from day one. I don't think that Twitter and Facebook had that governance in place from day one.

Jimmy: What's interesting about that is on a personal level, when I think about my values and things that I think are important.

In terms of a real authority and power, I'm one of ten members of the board. That's the extent of my power, plus my public presence, which gives me more influence than a lot of other board members in my position. But the truth is, control is not something I actually have . . . there's been a few little things here and there where I think I would have decided differently from staff. And I think this is horrible, or it's like: 'Oh, okay. Well, I would have done that differently, but actually I see the other side and it's fine.' So I've been very lucky that the organization hasn't sort of struck off in a bizarre direction.

And I do think that is about the full scale of the way it all works with the community, and the structures within the community, and all of the things that we designed very early on being fairly robust over time.

The Wikipedia community, I would say, is slightly left of centre, but they're not going to call people white supremacists because that's quite an extreme thing to say. Somebody put it in and somebody removed it very quickly. It was not a huge deal. It's just the noise of Wikipedia. You could be critical. Why does Wikipedia allow that kind of noise? Okay, that's a valid question, and I've got a good answer for it, but it's not like suddenly I'm fighting against a community who's gone radically left wing or radically right wing. We haven't been taken over by alt-right trolls or anything like that. That's good, and it's healthy that the system is reasonably robust, and obviously there's no guarantee that it will always stay so, but there's a lot of really sensible people, and so you feel comfortable. I sleep at night.

And I think, if somebody says: 'Oh, it's terrible about your Wikimedia.'

'Oh, what do you mean?'

'I hear that it's been taken over by total right wingers.'

I'm like: 'Oh, dear!' No. I feel that's not true, actually. And it isn't true.

Damian: I take a metaphor from the physical world. I think America is the epicentre of the boomtown. And what we've seen with the internet is this rise of pioneers, in the early days, who came in and set foundations, created community, failed, moved on slightly, built something else.

And some of the empires that we're seeing today are Facebook, Wikipedia, those sort of places. But I think we're going to go through a transformation in the cityscape of the internet, where we're going to see a lot more of the sort of strip malls disappearing as advertising revenue disappears. And more and more, I think we'll be moving to different revenue models. Subscriptions will be one part of it, but I don't know that I want to have a hundred subscriptions. What do you think? What do you think in twenty years from now is going to be the cityscape of the internet? How do you think it would look in terms of business models or community?

Jimmy: I think it's really hard to predict. There's a lot of different things that might happen.

I was on the internet which was academic and small. I knew there was America Online and Prodigy and CompuServe. And there was a belief, which I think was not entirely invalid, that whoever got biggest fast enough would win, and that it was going to be a monopoly business. Why would you sign up to AOL versus CompuServe? Well, you sign up for AOL because all your friends are on AOL, and that's your starting environment. There is no internet, in a sense. It's just that.

We dodged a bullet there. I don't think it was absolutely guaranteed that the internet was going to become the dominant online access, versus a company that managed a whole big process. Now maybe I'm wrong, maybe it was too hard for one company to scale. But I can envision if a company were smart enough, if AOL were smart enough to forego revenue, and encourage other companies, they'd say to whoever the predecessor of Amazon would have been: 'Come and set up your store here, and we'll give you all the tools. And we're going to lose massive money doing it.' It might have ended up that we were all on AOL, and a single company would have controlled the whole thing.

But we didn't end up in that world. And whether that was ever a real alternative or not, I don't know. I actually think it was possible that we could have ended up in that equilibrium.

And so similarly today, when I look at various changes

in the landscape, I do think there are interesting ways that we might end up in some kind of bad corner solution.

And then there's a lot of interesting ways where we end up still with a diverse, open internet that is the dominant platform, and it is a place that is neutral and everybody can join and so on.

I generally tend to agree with you. But I also have some concern that I might just be predicting the future based on what I hope is true.

See, if what I hope is true comes true, and I do think a large part of it will . . . I do think we'll move away from advertising-only business models. I don't think they're healthy for everything. I mean, for some things, fine, whatever. But I've been doing a lot around journalism. I've got my new project which is premiering, which is about communities and journalism and so on.

But one of my big concerns about journalism is that the advertising-only business model has been incredibly destructive to quality journalism, and the reason is quite obvious. The incentive that it puts in front of publishers in an era of programmatic advertising is just clickbait: as many eyeballs, as many pages as possible. Attract the right audience for five seconds and show them the high-value ad. It's basically a race to the bottom, clickbait-y content. And then serious publishers struggle, because serious content costs a lot of money to produce.

Meaningful things that change people's lives cost a lot of money to produce.

If *The Guardian* has a senior reporter working for three

weeks on a story, and that story is important, and it moves the needle, and it gets a lot of attention . . . and if at the same time, a clickbait-y publisher publishes a listicle, as they call it, '23 Cat Photos, And Number 7 Will Make You Cry' that some millennial intern made in three hours of an afternoon, and they're clever and funny, and it makes the same amount of page views and the same amount of money, then *The Guardian* has to look at that and goes: 'This business model is not working for us. We should just be hiring a lot of funny young kids to write fluffy content, because it's cheap and it gets eyeballs.' As opposed to what I'm really excited about is we've seen the *New York Times*, their subscriptions have gone from a million to three million in the last couple of years.

That, for me, is one of the most positive little indicators in society that, actually, people are willing to pay. And how do you sell subscriptions? You have to make a difference to people's lives. So people don't pay the *New York Times* because they saw something that made them click and they wasted fifteen minutes of their life clicking on 'You Won't Believe What This Child Star Looks Like Now'. They read a piece, and they thought: 'Wow, that's important. I need to support this. This should exist. I should pay for this.' And the fact that we're starting to see subscription models take off in journalism is really important.

In a lot of areas I think that can be very important. And a lot of the advertising-only stuff is going to end up being just . . . you won't get quality there. You'll just get noise, and I think that matters. I think people are going to be interested in saying yeah, actually, I want to pay for this because it's worth paying for. Sometimes people talk about, in all the journalism, that the industry made a strategic mistake by giving away their stuff for free, and now people are used to it and they don't want to pay for the news.

I think that's actually wrong. I think that's too simplistic a view. It was really hard to pay. So the more we have app models and easy payment methods, where people can just go yeah, this is worth it, I'm going to pay for it. And they don't have to pull out their credit card, and they don't have to type in all the digits and then worry about security and all that. The more people can just go yeah, that's great, I want to buy that, out of an impulse purchase, then they will.

I agree with your overall view that people paying for content – people paying for services of various kinds – is likely to be a more dominant piece of landscape than it has been. And I think that's a good thing.

●●●

11: Lessons from Amsterdam

Part of the WeTransfer story is being from elsewhere. The usual tech narrative stresses Silicon Valley. This one's going to introduce Holland. You might have heard of it: flat place.

Holland is a trading nation. You can very easily pitch, convince the necessary folk, and start a business that buys cheap hotel rooms and sells them at a 10 per cent mark-up. Look no further than Booking.com. This is the sort of thing that works, traditionally, in Holland.

It's ten times harder to convince a tradesman to invest in a cultural business. All the activities WeTransfer had become involved in during its short lifespan were, in some shape or form, involved in the design, art, film or culture community. This could have been seen as a hindrance. These subjects were sometimes treated with suspicion in the business community of our home country. On the positive side of things, Holland doesn't let anyone get away with bullshit.

WeTransfer had to offer something real. Even at an early stage, we had to stress trust. Anybody creating anything and entrusting it to a third party to send should feel trust, but the file sharing world of yesteryear had left a bad taste in people's mouths. The Royal Mail, FedEx, DHL are all organizations that rely 100 per cent on trust 'when it absolutely, positively has to be there overnight' (FedEx, 1981).

It's impossible to argue against the following: Americans believe Europe is more grounded. It's in the traditions and customs. For them, it's an inescapable trait, and in the move-fast-and-break-things world of Silicon Valley, anything traditional or grounded is looked upon askance.

We're not the only practitioners. As mentioned, in Amsterdam, across town from us, is Booking.com, the biggest company in Holland and perhaps the biggest holiday company in the world. The company is run from the canals, not from some glistening campus in Oakland with acres of parking, or some far-off, walled-in destination outside San Francisco, reachable by a fleet of private buses. Booking.com chose to stay, even though their row of canal houses alongside one another is the definition of impractical. There's no parking. It's difficult to access.

But something's working: the quality of life that Amsterdam provides is high.

The company that sits on the water is an aberration.

Headquartered in Amsterdam, with 12,000 employees and 197 offices in 70 countries elsewhere, the business was founded by Geert-Jan Bruinsma. In 2005 Booking.com was sold for $133 million and in 2011 went on to make $1.1 billion profit. By 2016 they were spending three times that in advertising on Google alone.

Companies can't help but take attributes from their place

of origin. Amsterdam's a beautiful village masquerading as a city. Even if you're trying to get three projects off the ground, you can have a life that incorporates kids. Often Amsterdam's beauty wins out and attracts top European talent. Happiness is the most important metric there when raising a family. That unit of measurement tends to be used in business as well.

Growing a business here is comparable to raising a Dutch kid. Good things happen when you start from a safe place. Good things happen when a focus is put on quality of life, when values are stressed from a young age. English is second nature to everyone. Raising a child or a business in a traditional trading nation means focus is put on the outside world. There is never a sense of insularity. Pragmatism abounds. Frugality and transparency are stressed. You are taught to know where you stand.

There is less a sense of 'I'll do whatever it takes' than 'This is who I am.'

As WeTransfer grew, we realized it would be easy to springboard from Amsterdam – just as we eventually did – while keeping a set of values intact. Trusting our users was at the top of that list.

And what about the money in Holland? Here was another place where our Dutch values showed through.

By 2014, we'd begun to break even at WeTransfer. That said, there were still many months that went by when we were living hand to mouth. We were occasionally dependent on an unsustainable financial system known as 'people mistakenly paying us twice'. This didn't happen much. Only once did we receive a cheque twice for the same amount from an advertiser. It certainly helped keep the lights on. (We did repay them.)

The team had grown to around 25 people. Our design studio, Present Plus, employed 16 people. We were beginning to get a lot of interest from investors about WeTransfer.

As the interest continued to grow, we decided to employ a banker to help manage the process.

What was very clear by 2015 was that everyone felt they had put enough blood, sweat and tears into this project. We all wanted to release some of the pressure, so we went ahead and hired that banker.

We went through the usual routine of accepting their flattery. This was a moment where we edged out of our trusted safety zone and began to encounter the values of the outside world. Bankers have perfected ways to woo small businesses. But there was still a nagging feeling that our banker did not truly understand our particular business. It didn't feel so Dutch.

He didn't grasp the advertising model and certainly lacked a feel for the vision. This courtship lasted about two to three weeks, until we had spent enough time with the bankers – in particular the most junior person on their team – and a crucial point was becoming clear.

WeTransfer is a cultural business. It's a business with more than one business model. It required a different way of thinking. Normally I can get people to understand WeTransfer in around thirty minutes. I don't need to speak fast. I can convey its mission, values, goals and points of differentiation.

The bankers were a tough crowd. They were a litmus test. Was it difficult to convey our goals because they didn't make sense? Or because bankers just weren't wired to see the world this way?

We went out to San Francisco. We flew to New York City. We searched out allies all over the place. Eventually, we hit on a team of venture capitalists that seemed to get us. It wasn't a chore to explain the company to them. They flew in to meet us. Then they flew their entire company over. Things were going well.

Picture us all at dinner at the Golden Pheasant restaurant in Amsterdam, a cavernous warehouse, lined with tables covered in pristine white linen, situated on the river. The warehouse was stuffed with classic cars. Our idea of a single investor had now ballooned. It felt like we were surrounded by twenty, and they all really wanted to invest.

Scratch that. It felt like they wanted to rabidly invest, like they were about to foam at the mouth. *Investment*. They impressed that point upon us. We appeared to have completely skipped dating and were straight into a marriage ceremony – and not at a registry office. There were going to be lots of people at this ceremony.

Champagne popped. Someone leaned over to me and promised me a golf trip somewhere. Pebble Beach? Who just leans over and says let's take a golf trip? Maybe it involved getting there via helicopter? Helicopters were mentioned, as were huge deals and bad jokes. Some of the people at the table had started Lycos or Netscape or perhaps even the internet. Did someone just lean over and tell me they'd invented the internet? Maybe while playing golf they'd tell me how they did it? That's how big they were.

The deal was done – nearly. As they sat in our boardroom, we received a pep talk from our banker in the room across the hall. Trust me, he said. This was actually a form of role play. They're going to say this and then you will look surprised – and make sure it's a genuine look of surprise. Then you'll come back with a counter-offer.

The whole interaction had sunk to the level of some amateur production of *Glengarry Glen Ross*. Besides, that kind of 'Always be closing' routine didn't play so well in Amsterdam.

But, generally, this moment signified a great change. This was it. We would no longer have to beg our suppliers to pay us on time. We would no longer have to cross our fingers and hope our sales team was always nearing the end of a killer month. It felt good. We would be set.

As per usual, there were complications. The next morning, when I got to the office, Stefan Verkerk (one of the founding team members), Bas and Nalden all looked up at me like someone had died. I guess, in a way, someone had.

'You're not gonna believe this,' Stefan said, 'but they pulled out. We got an email this morning saying something came up. They aren't returning our calls, but we're ninety-nine per cent sure the deal is off.'

The deal was indeed off. We never heard from them again. Ever.

In hindsight, I realize this is what happened when we strayed too far from our Dutch roots, when we began to believe in another way of handling money.

Apart from the broken promises, the bluster, the exaggerations and outright lies, what annoyed me most was that I had already learned – or so I thought – the hard lesson of business from my career so far, especially my time working in Russia: 'Don't spend the money until the money is in the bank.'

Be Dutch.

Two months later, a new deal was on the table. This time it came from a European venture capitalist firm who were smart, pragmatic and good at listening. We willingly signed with them and still work with them to this day. No talk of Pebble Beach or helicopters.

I don't believe in luck, destiny or fate, but serendipity might belong in a category of its own. Had we signed with the original party of golfing *Glengarry Glen Ross* men, I'm convinced we would be in a very different place than where we are today. Our current VCs have supported the way we think. They've trusted us. Even today they understand the way we work, act, behave, communicate, and fall in and out of love with ideas. They've helped us to grow to where we are. Partnerships like this aren't marriages – it's not a worthwhile comparison – but there is a dynamic at play here.

VCs are shaped by their culture. Their way of viewing the world is often set. Wherever they fly in the world, whichever restaurant they choose, or local language they might speak, they're usually bringing with them the VC culture of Silicon Valley.

We were lucky to sidestep it. It might well be because they aren't based in the Valley.

Who knows?

Dealing with VCs outside the culture of Silicon Valley re-inforced the belief that we need to tell new stories. I don't mean that in a cheesy marketing sense. We need to actually come up with new origin stories for tech companies. The one we're clinging to isn't really working. Let me take a moment in this narrative, at a time when WeTransfer is steadily growing in the background, to explain what I mean.

There are clichéd routes to success in every field. Some kid, right now, has spent years kicking an old football against a wall in a run-down neighbourhood and is about to be given a chance at an academy far from his parents. This kid, with his talent honed, will go on to play for a small club, a larger club, a youth team, a European club, his national team and, finally, appear in a Verizon commercial explaining soccer to the American masses.

We recognize all sorts of clichéd trajectories. In the tech world, in the US, the trajectory doesn't stray much from a story we've been told a thousand times. But as tech matures, it's clear the mythical trajectory is flawed and the mono-story is getting tired.

There are different ways than the track publicized by the tech press and conference scene. WeTransfer didn't do an angel round. Ashton Kutcher and his money were nowhere in sight. We didn't raise 200 million in Series A. We don't have a billion-dollar valuation going into an IPO. When it comes to many of the traditional markers, some of which capsize young companies, we weren't interested.

Perhaps now is a good time to stress the polyphonic way of telling tech stories. We need plenty of new origin stories, and plenty of different people telling them. The old ones are still beneficial to some, and employees get to tell their friends an understood trajectory: 'We just got a 1.2 billion dollar valuation, and Peter Thiel just invested, and we've purchased seventeen companies this year.' That is the old folk tale everyone's heard before: raising money, valuation, acquisitions.

But there are other stories that arise from other places – like Holland. One story happens to be ours: bootstrapped, driven in a different way, intent on giving ad space away.

(This is why I see us as closer to a Vermont ice cream company than our tech brothers and sisters. I see us as part of a culture of pleasure and free-sharing, rather than another pestering element of what I increasingly view as the drudge internet: social media upkeep; compulsive, anxiety-stirring Instagram trawls).

The new narratives can come from different places – again, Holland – or different mindsets. I've tried to gather some of the voices I admire most in this book – Aspiration Bank, DuckDuckGo, Wikipedia and, coming up, Omidyar – showing us a different mode of behaviour for VCs.

One narrative I like is that companies that form elsewhere in the world cultivate different values. There's now a broad international set of flavours when it comes to values in the tech world.

The well-disguised rapaciousness and glee that comes with data-trampling might not make the top ten where we came from. In Amsterdam, we didn't have to conform to this narrative. In Europe, it's difficult to raise money, especially sums comparable to American money, so we were forced to be very careful about how we spent ours. We had to be careful with that banker.

There are different stories to tell when it comes to how fast you grow. Sometimes it's better to embrace manageable growth, rather than trying to scale that terrifying beanstalk.

The narrative exported from Silicon Valley is completely bereft of the benefits of failure – unless there's a useful semi-failure, like Steve Jobs' expulsion from Apple before his triumphant return. We found true benefits in failure in Amsterdam: ugly, informative failure, but never tied to the expectations of outlandish infusions of cash. We had room to fail, experiment, question, without the push of investors.

There's a tension, of course. The Europeans would love to have a little bit of Silicon Valley. (In the UK, it would be much better to have a valley than a Silicon Roundabout, the least glamorous place on earth: grungy, grimy and grey.)

Europe is a tough market because of the overriding cautiousness. People are afraid of risking everything and losing everything. This might not make for such a gung-ho narrative for the winners: it doesn't play into the idea of the heroic ur-Thiel, rising from the ranks of mere humans to become a rich superman, a lesser-known Marvel hero. But it's time, as we reconsider the landscape, to examine the benefits of this caution: the anti-sexy tech growth model. Growth without glamour.

Holland is an extreme example, and we learned from our corner of the world.

In the US, you'd start worrying if you lost the equivalent of a hundred dollars. In the UK, you'd start worrying if you lost ten pounds. In Holland, alarm bells would sound if you lost one euro. I know Dutch people who could happily spend the day on the phone to save forty euros on a flight. To be fair, in these cases, I feel like an outsider: my Britishness, my burgeoning Americanness, rears up. Surely, losing hours of your time is not worth this. But still, the principle at the core is: I'm not going to let our money go. Just try speaking those words in California.

One of the other lessons we learned from Amsterdam was to embed yourself in a community, surround yourself with other types of people, graphic designers and artists, and work at this, pull yourself away from the allure of the tech-vacuum.

There are challenges – like finding good local talent – but use what's around, use the strength of the city, the allure of the place, to find a different kind of person.

Offer trust.

What are the deeper issues here? It's great to attach yourself to the values of a place and what a place has traditionally exemplified. As mentioned, Amsterdam afforded us canals and a good lifestyle for kids. But we have to go further.

What the literature of the tech journals often shies away from is the increasing importance of moving yourself away from the people who have banded together to form the social culture of investment. Don't replicate the Silicon Valley mind-set in all these outposts around the world. Don't install its values in other cities. Money is only part of the story.

The same energy put into seeking out money for the future needs to be put into finding a group who will help seek out

167

ideas for the future. Why would an AI or medical services company align itself with thinkers and artists? Well, good question, but historically the role of the questioning artist has served well.

VCs could learn from the creative community in the same way we have. We need more VCs looking at some sort of big picture, placing long-term bets in order to make a difference. So long as the VC world only believes in the Getty model of 'get rich quick and become a philanthropist later' nothing will change. If VC culture remains in Silicon Valley, at the very least its values need to be dragged to a new place, a higher ground.

One way of solving the idea of VC culture is by staying away from it. (I'd recommend Holland.) It was important to talk about money and what money meant to us, how it came to us, how it was refused us, and what money made of us. We learned the lessons that were offered with fast money, and the lessons that came with what we ended up with – slow money.

We've benefited from moving outside the circles and the attendant values of Big Tech, and it's from outside these circles and values that the lessons of the future will come. It's a good place to forge connection, to invite people back in: a plurality of voices, thought, ideas. After all, from what we've recently seen, the status quo in tech is an unempathetic world.

We've got a problem. We build products that cause harm, erode privacy. It's worth asking: What kind of culture encourages this behaviour?

Growing our company in Amsterdam meant we didn't need

to sever our connection to thought, art, compassion, empathy. We didn't have to become a company that doesn't value the totality of human interaction and fixate instead on a lesser version. We rejected the tech echo chamber – I've lived it, I've seen it – in which coders and developers are bused into campuses, all the while telling themselves they're agents of the counterculture.

In her famous essay about Google buses in San Francisco, author Rebecca Solnit comments on this strange, time-worn story the tech world keeps telling itself. 'Their confusion may issue from Silicon Valley's own favourite stories about itself,' she wrote in the *London Review of Books* back in 2014. 'These days in TED Talks and tech-world conversation, commerce is described as art and as revolution and huge corporations are portrayed as agents of the counterculture.'

She's got a point. It's a good warning to tech. She sees the real story behind the myth. She knows the origin story is getting tired. It's not even told truthfully. Tech might have been different back in the day:

> . . . briefly, in the popular tech Genesis story according to which Apple emerged from a garage somewhere at the south end of the San Francisco Peninsula, not yet known as Silicon Valley. But Google set itself up with the help of a $4.5 million dollar government subsidy, and Apple became a giant corporation that begat multimillion-dollar advertising campaigns and overseas sweatshops and the rest that you already know. Facebook, Google, eBay and Yahoo (though not Apple) belong to the conservative anti-environmental

political action committee ALEC (the American Legislative Exchange Council).'

What is the actual culture of Silicon Valley? Does it really beat what we've got in Amsterdam? In Europe? They are able to push forward with intrusion, tracking, data mining, erosion. And the fetishization of disruption above all else, the cult of disruption that leads to the question: moving where and breaking what?

I get this image of the disrupters now, looking out across the landscape today: seeing information without facts, foreign influence, hate speech and endless data mining.

I'd take a view of the canals over that any day.

12: Sometimes New Isn't Best

How many companies get a chance to redefine themselves? WeTransfer did. After we settled some of our money issues, we knew we needed to focus on what was at the core of the company – here we were, lucky to be a transfer service that would last and be relevant as long as people needed to shift their ideas to another person.

We'd fostered a fan base with artists, the community that mattered most to us. We'd set out to become valuable to people who depended on the transfer of information, who built projects a step at a time, whose big ideas needed big files. If we played our cards right and truly made this community happy, they would never stop transferring. We had their loyalty. We had their trust. Now we wanted to help them produce.

There was a prolonged span of time when we were able to look around the cultural landscape and say: Wouldn't it be cool if this existed, or that existed? (This could have been the result of getting a little money.) We were keen to start projects and conscious of setting a tone. Transfer meant things got built, ideas were broadcast. We'd made short films. Maybe it would make sense to start a radio station? We thought about the time-honoured ways that information and thought were transferred. We thought about the transfer of ideas from professor to student. Maybe down the road we could start a university? Someone's got to start a university. Why not? Student debt was already getting out of hand. (We started one. More on that later.)

The way we viewed and treated the site changed. We had created a space for discovery, and in order to ensure it remained interesting and substantial we needed to curate it. The space needed great advertising to help keep the site alive, and beautiful visuals to help keep visitors engaged. It was around this time that we began to recognize a distinction between 'great' advertising and what else was out there. Some argued there could never be such a thing as great advertising. Advertising, they said, was always a scam. And yes, in some ways it is. But by that point, we'd seen our competitors destroy their bond of trust with their users. They'd decided to forego obvious advertising for the data mining model. We'd seen the reach of peak spam. We'd seen all the different and nasty ways advertising was cloaking itself. Advertising could be something different. Maybe not 'great', but better.

Many people referred to our ads as the 'billboards of the web'. Why was that? We weren't evangelical about the healing power of advertising. But we also knew it didn't have to be a drag. We applied rules to the advertising we showcased. Less is more. Limit the amount of copy. Keep the messaging short and to the point, and attract people visually. If this advice sounds like a voice from the past, you're right. These rules were lifted from the advertising greats.

Six words or less is ideal.
Get noticed. Don't distract.
Billboards don't do direct response.
Be smart.
Don't say it. Show it.
Avoid repetition.
Keep it simple, stupid.

Convincing online advertisers to follow these simple rules was always a struggle. But convincing artists was easy. The more creative the individual or organization, the easier it was for them to understand why this was so important.

Throughout this process we had a feeling our approach was not bad business. Pivoting towards the outside world and working with artistic communities wasn't going to sting us. If anything, this announcement of our values meant that users were often pleasantly surprised by what else we were up to. We weren't putting our funds into surveillance. We weren't putting our money and energy towards a kind of Ayn Randian zero sum view of the world. We weren't looking to crush, co-opt or monopolize.

In our own small way, we wanted to change the larger definition of trust in the tech world. The focus was put on useful collaborations, rather than data mining and ploys to harvest more from users.

We kept interrogating the definition of sharing. Where had it come from? How could we define it for ourselves? If we asked others to share, shouldn't that mean we could do the same? The transparency we believed in went both ways.

WeTransfer had become a service for the curious. We'd attracted millions of users. These people naturally embraced the idea of sharing ideas. We just helped the ideas along their journey. We did have a bit of luck, too. We were on the right side of history. Our business had changed and grown, but the context had changed too.

What else was happening with the other file sharing sites? Good question. It wasn't a great scene out there. In the years following our birth, the file sharing world started to implode. MegaUpload, run by the king of all internet narcissists, Kim Dotcom, was shut down for promoting piracy and plagiarism. YouSendIt made the gross error of engaging an advertising agency and heeding their advice to change their name to Hightail. (What's a hightail? Who would want to have a hightail?) RapidShare rapidly disappeared. The less said the better.

WeTransfer sailed on, promoting creativity and quality, at peace with the record industry instead of hunted by their lawyers. We had always fostered close ties with musicians and music industry employees. Our friends worked in the music business. The service was built for people like them. But the dream of partnering with triple A musicians to distribute music using our service seemed distant.

We were no longer in fight or flight mode. It was time to

collaborate and put some of these ideas in motion, especially since we looked around at how the competition was embarking on larger projects.

In 2013, our friends across the water at BitTorrent had partnered with *Vice* and Madonna to release a short 17-minute film entitled *secretprojectrevolution* through their platform. We watched closely as attention spiked and waned. Their transparent move to purchase credibility was greeted with disdain by the creative community.

Like many larger companies, BitTorrent has over the years partnered with artists, film-makers and celebrities to help grow their business. We were envious they had managed to get buy-in to develop this strategy of big bets. Luckily for us, the strategy of big bets was typically short term. They tended to die off quickly. Instead of making big one-off bets, we stayed focused on setting a tone, piece by piece, artist by artist.

We didn't have to ponder which direction to take. Serendipity stepped in. A certain god-like purple figure entered our world. We tried to form a relationship with Prince. Who wouldn't want to form a relationship with that guy? It died out. And then, surprisingly, it was reborn.

In March 2015, and in his typically philanthropic state of mind, Prince tried to convince Live Nation to allow him to email their entire database a WeTransfer link to download the new album from Judith Hill, the 31-year-old daughter of a Japanese piano player and the star of *20 Feet from Stardom*. Live Nation said no.

Regardless, Prince uploaded Judith's album to WeTransfer

and shared it via Twitter. This single action started a chain reaction of events. First, it demonstrated that people were able to copy and paste short links to hosted music files. This action prompted the music industry to use our service more than ever to distribute, not just to help create, the music. It revealed an altruistic side of the cut-throat music industry. It inspired others, including Moby, to share new tracks and entire back catalogues of music.

This was a direction we'd have to take. And here we were again, embracing a fusty old concept that had been left behind in the mad scramble to release pirated music. What was our problem? Did this go back to us being Dutch? Did we just have a terrible problem shaking this sense of ethics? We built a music relations team to help facilitate the legal distribution of music to our growing community. They were creative. They wanted to share. They believed this could be the right way – even though it resembled the way people had always shared. With permission.

Oh, and what was I talking about when it came to post-secondary education?

In 2016 we launched the University of the Underground, one of the world's first completely free MA programmes, which featured degrees in experience design and design thinking.

The process was intuitive. The artist Nelly Ben Hayoun helped set up a list of what the university would offer. There would be a focus on what she called social dreaming, critical design, social actions, politics, theatrical practices, film, music and experiential practices. The university aimed to provide toolkits for members of the public to actively participate in revealing power structures within institutions.

The University of the Underground supports unconventional research and practices that challenge the formulation of culture, the manufacture and commodities of knowledge. And – importantly for us – it's a form of education that goes across borders and beyond nation states.

Seventeen students joined in the first year. The ambition is to have multiple campuses, with a strong US presence, to counter the ridiculousness of tuition fees and the increasing uncertainty of job security.

Through Nelly's work we could see that the transfer of ideas was important in the context of a one-to-one relationship.

'The internet is a fantastic tool, and a platform,' she told me recently, 'but this will never replace one-to-one tutoring and mentoring. The internet is a good platform to showcase your work, but for me the best platform is experience. Experience the event.'

More and more, it was integral for us – a fledgling internet company – to work with thinkers like Nelly who were focused on what she called 'beyond-internet' – what happens after the screen.

'The problem with the internet now is that a lot of it is [about] the monopoly of platform, like Instagram, Facebook and others,' she told me. 'I don't think the next revolution will come from there.'

I tend to agree.

FINALLY, SOME ICE CREAM

I've mentioned offline values a number of times. With Nelly at the University of the Underground stressing the importance of what happened outside the online world, I looked around at the companies that have provided guidance to me.

I'd often ask myself one of the most elemental questions: What is good business? What is its essence?

I've spent my life looking at different companies, weighing them up, assessing, so I'll choose a deceptively easy target. Everybody loves Ben & Jerry's. You'd be hard pressed to find anyone who would say something like: 'I simply despise Ben & Jerry's. I *despise* the salted caramel core. How could they body-shame monkeys into believing they're chunky?'

From the beginning, in 1978, at a Vermont gas station, Ben & Jerry's has embodied good business – so good that, in 2000, Unilever bought them for about $326 million in cash, or $43.60 a share. Unilever made the purchase but also agreed to something called the 'social mission process'. This basically meant they had to continue to fulfil exactly Ben & Jerry's stated mission. It's good business. The key point was that Unilever agreed to commit 7.5 per cent of Ben & Jerry's profits to a foundation. Unilever was compelled to refrain from cutting jobs. The ice cream wouldn't get messed with.

It makes sense. People love them for it, and Phish Food still tastes good, even if the band it's named after leaves a bad taste in your mouth after one of their twelve-minute guitar solos.

More importantly, the story reads well on any page, including this one. Ben & Jerry's wanted to make ice cream, and then they told compelling stories around it. Some individual flavours were attached to specific causes, but their starting point was good dessert, period. They didn't need an external idea, like B Corp, to enhance what was already there.

A while ago I was with the then CEO of Ben & Jerry's, Jostein Solheim, in San Francisco. Nineteen years after the Unilever purchase, little has changed. The governance they set out when they sold the company still states something along the lines of: 'You can't touch the brands. You can't change the way our ice cream is made. You can't change the way we treat employees, and you can't change stuff we do with our mission.'

They installed a governing body that does not report to the Unilever board. The CEO of Amnesty International was made responsible. That's the kind of strong governance most companies, including my own, don't have. I mean, I wish we did. The structure they put in place enforced the future of Ben & Jerry's.

Somehow, even in the world we must live in, this ice cream company was able to make a compelling argument to keep doing what it set out to do. They built trust and then remained determined to keep it. That's brilliant business. For me it's the benchmark. That's what we're trying to do. We're not there yet. We haven't fully Ben-&-Jerry'd, but it's a good goal.

Often we hear of smaller companies subsumed into larger companies and irrevocably changed. They lose their aim and their ability to hold on to any original values. Ben & Jerry's aren't just a success. They are one of the healthiest businesses in the whole of Unilever. Ben & Jerry's have been fundamentally changing the way Unilever has approached GM. They've forced their parent company to take a different approach to organic and fair trade products. They've helped a cumbersome, huge parent company pay attention to the zeitgeist. In response, Unilever has changed many of its other products.

It's brilliant: these two little hippies who knew little about business somehow unleashed a wave of change. It's built on a trust embedded in the company. They're not faking it. It's not a slogan on a bottle of Innocent. And look what's just happened. It's become a good story to tell and retell. There's a tangible warmth.

Let's switch over to tech. Feel the chill, especially if you consider Comcast and Verizon and Spectrum, the three companies that dominate internet business in the US. Around 380 million people have access to the internet via this trio. Does anyone feel warmth towards them? Does anyone like these companies? Does anybody out there profess *love* for them, or admire what they've been able to do, the changes they've been able to install, the values they embody? Is there any sort of value system that should be exported from these companies?

Does anyone drive down to Tupelo, Mississippi, to visit the former offices of a small cable operator known as American Cable – the company that would one day become the Comcast behemoth?

If a little ice cream operation like Ben & Jerry's can touch the hearts and minds of so many people, why can't these three? If you think about it, the opportunity that Verizon, Comcast and Spectrum have to positively influence our lives is huge. I cannot exist today without them.

You might be tethered to them too – or companies very much like them in other parts of the world.

Why don't they? That may seem like a naive three-word question, but let's press at it with a little more force. Why don't they? Which tech company is fulfilling the role of a Ben & Jerry's? Who engages on that sort of level? I'd argue you'd be hard pressed to find anyone. Facebook would love to be included in the same sentence as Ben & Jerry's. People love certain elements about Facebook, but look at the wince on the faces of your friends when Facebook is dropped into the conversation.

Do people really want to make pilgrimages to Facebook's HQ? Perhaps. Perhaps they're looking to recover some of their hidden data.

No one yells out: 'I love Facebook. I love spending all my time on it. I love that feeling I get when I know it's doing something that will fundamentally enhance the world.' Facebook has become, for most thinking people, a grudging chore. You must maintain connection with it. The world dictates you do so.

I know what you're thinking. I'd like Facebook and Comcast a lot better if they came from the freezer and had pieces of cookie dough embedded in them. I was arguing this with their CEO in San Francisco: it's difficult for a tech company to elicit the same sort of response or reaction, or interaction, without having a physical presence.

You go to the fridge, pull out a pint, imagine the taste, read the packaging, follow the story. The physical presence is associated with fun and pleasure and tasting good. Comcast has got nothing like that.

It could be viewed as a deficit. Actually, this sort of relationship is a possibility for the tech sector. But we haven't managed to produce an experience that really does capture hearts. (I'm hesitant to use the phrase 'hearts and minds' with all its connotations of wars in Iraq and Vietnam, but the two terms do go together, kind of like Cherry and Garcia.) The tech world gets your mind.

It's rare we get your heart, and even rarer that we keep it. I don't mean slavish devotion here. I'm talking about a triple prong – transparency, a company wreathed in a good purpose, and also a pleasurable user experience. Ice cream is pretty much the greatest user experience. There are different, subtle strands of trust woven together here. It matters.

At the moment, I'd say the warmest tech company is Apple. Apple has managed to move into the physical world. But that's because they have a physical presence. Apple set a benchmark in retail. Most people like going to the Apple store. It's beautiful: they like the products laid out on those big, flat wooden tables. The experience is phenomenal in terms of retail and their generosity towards space.

The pleasure of going into the Apple store is there's about ten things set out in front of you with lots of airy space. Free Wi-Fi. They offer up a strategic generosity. But is generosity trust?

Maybe that's what it is. Trust is the gift I give to you. You can't ask it of me. Generosity is the thing that you can give to me. You can be generous. You can't just suddenly become trustworthy. With Apple, a generosity comes through. But have they gained and kept our trust?

Another interesting angle is confidence. Apple has shown a confidence that not many other companies have. I would argue we have a similar brand of confidence. We have a whole screen dedicated to the transfer. We only fill it with one thing. There aren't a lot of other websites confident enough to do that. The goal of the web is usually to fill the screen up with shit. You don't know what you want, so I'm going to give you tons of stuff to choose from. That's not confidence.

And it's certainly not trust.

13: Going to California Doesn't Always Mean San Francisco

Amidst all of our new projects and collaborations, WeTransfer transformed again. We decided to go international.

I agreed to move to the US. I wasn't banished from the kingdom. (I don't think.) Rather, I went to set up an office on the west coast while the board started looking for a new CEO in Amsterdam.

We had reconfigured the business, begun collaborative relationships all over the world, and it felt like the right time for more simplicity. We were one entity, WeTransfer, instead of three, and money was no longer a pressing issue. This gave us the chance to step back and survey what we'd become. We got to consider where we'd been and, in a slightly more disconcerting continuation, we had to figure out what was next.

Just as British musicians have always aspired to follow in the footsteps of the Beatles and crack the US charts, almost every European start-up has dreamed of conquering America. We've always been particularly obsessed with the place.

Success in the US isn't always possible, easy or worthwhile. But try telling that to ambitious Europeans.

Whatever you think of the current government, the US is the real deal: the country with the most Nobel laureates; the largest number of Olympians and VCs; the country where people either make it or break it. We'd reached 20 per cent penetration of the Dutch market, and now recognized that achievement as the point where we needed to cross the ocean.

We were – if I do say so myself – the darlings of the European creative industry. We were profitable. And once in a while, in moments of outrageous confidence, we thought to ourselves: Imagine if we could reach 20 per cent of the US market. Imagine if we could go there without changing our fundamental values.

That's the other point that doesn't get stressed enough. It's easy to announce you're heading to the US. It's not always easy to choose the right place – to find the staging ground to continue with the same purpose and ethical drive. We could easily have set up in San Francisco within the crowd of tech companies fighting for column inches in *TechCrunch*. We too could have enjoyed unlimited investor meet-ups, company dry-cleaning services and in-office three-star Michelin chefs. But, increasingly, moving to the US doesn't mean California. And moving to California doesn't necessarily mean San Francisco. We'd had a taste of Silicon Valley VC culture, and it wasn't right for us.

San Francisco is an amazing environment. Coming from Europe, the climate alone is both very attractive and weirdly European. The bay's microclimate offers expats the chance to moan about the weather every day. Vineyards lie within arm's reach. Mountains rise, forests sprawl, and in between are lakes and hiking trails. If it seems like a perfect holiday destination, maybe it's best left for the holidays.

But from a work perspective things get complex: Commercial space is around $34 per sq/ft and project managers don't come cheap, with salaries of around $100,000 per year. Developers get $300,000 per year, sometimes more. Housing is on average 45 per cent more expensive than nearby Los Angeles. It is the most expensive city in the US – and probably the most screwed up, as it becomes richer and richer and more unequal.

'All this is changing the character of what was once a great city of refuge for dissidents, queers, pacifists and experimentalists,' Rebecca Solnit wrote in the *London Review of Books*. 'Like so many cities that flourished in the post-industrial era, it has become increasingly unaffordable over the past quarter-century, but still has a host of writers, artists, activists, environmentalists, eccentrics and others who don't work sixty-hour weeks for corporations – though we may be a relic population.'

If we wanted to export our kind of thinking to the US, we wanted some distance from where all that usual thinking was taking place. We didn't want to be part of the problem in San Francisco. And so, we went to the home of deep critical thinking and boundless community engagement.

Just kidding: we went to LA.

But hold on, LA is also more complicated than mere stereotypes. It's easy to laugh at Los Angeles, but look closer and there's something interesting happening within those city limits. Los Angeles was our landing spot. We could have done something completely out of the blue and set up in Missouri, but LA seemed radical enough.

Los Angeles still feels like it's on the cusp. When we arrived, unemployment was dropping. House prices were on the rise. Average wages were increasing. Areas such as Downtown Los Angeles were undergoing redevelopment. The architecture – I noticed this as a European on my first reconnaissance mission – is more varied than most cities. The city is diverse, and so big that twelve major US cities will fit snugly within its city limits.

We wouldn't be alone. Snapchat, Headspace, Dollar Shave Club, The Honest Company, TrueCar and 496 other tech start-ups were now all housed somewhere between Venice, Culver City and Marina Del Rey. Like a strange admission of surgical augmentation, this area had become known, perhaps stupidly, as Silicon Beach.

All of that worked in our favour (except the name). But it felt like there was a huge ethical customs check waiting for us. Could we export our Dutch values?

I had been visiting LA for a few years now and still found it a difficult city to pin down. It isn't the city that never sleeps, nor is it the cultural capital, nor is it the windy city, nor the motor city.

After a while in California, I began to see why it could be good for a company like WeTransfer. LA is the forgiving city. It's the city of reincarnation. We were still looking to bring about change in some small way. Our projects and collaborations were leading us in that direction. Nelly had given me a reading list from the University. It was full of writers who wanted change, who could foresee change. LA is the city most accepting of change. It's a good place to fail – in the best possible way. Here, people fail every day. Actors have shaped this city and, week in and week out, they have to audition. Ninety per cent of auditions end in failure. So it's fine. Failure's not personal. It's business. A city that understands the positive elements of failure is a great place for a start-up. Or for a company that is starting up afresh.

Just as important as room for experiments and failure was a feeling that being here helped us realize the growing importance of responsible tech. Suddenly we were surrounded by a cacophony of voices and opinions, expressed by all sorts of people, including those who found ways to deny the importance of responsible tech, or scoff, or loudly celebrate and justify the model of data extraction. In the US, the competing voices are piercing, clear, compelling and seductive.

'How can this be wrong when we're all doing it?' one might ask, while justifying her own data extraction attempts.

'How can this be bad when it's so exciting?'

'If the possibility is here, shouldn't we try?'

'Do not stand in the way,' ominous drop in tone, 'of the Internet of Things.'

The idea of responsible tech stands out when you move to a place where the latest tech trend cannot be wrong and the direction the Big Tech companies have set out for themselves is not only inevitable but always correct.

But we were heartened by a few responses in our new home. One was evident in our hiring process. We started to see millennials prioritizing the moral bearings of the company. Millennials: they actually care about whether or not the company is doing evil, being evil, and they're willing to adjust their priorities accordingly. This isn't just anecdotal. There's a growing slice of the workforce that does not want to work on dubious projects – somehow the appeal of designing, for instance, censorship tools for the Chinese government or tracking devices or the ability to listen in on private lives doesn't make their souls sing. Maybe it's a California thing, but change towards responsible tech is going to come from entrepreneurs. It will be driven by pressure from the people they hire – who might be wise to data extraction practices by now, who might have read some of the growing body of literature, who might actually be rebels, unlike the ones who just dress like rebels in Silicon Valley.

And they might want to look for meaning, both in terms of form and company purpose. This idea helped us in our thinking about where we would stand in relation to the user. I'd become interested in Sir Ken Robinson's ideas about 'flow'. I was immediately attracted to the ramifications for the business, so the concept became one of the most important pillars of WeTransfer.

The move to California helped clarify what flow meant, and how it could migrate from being a mere catchphrase to a company stance.

At its core, flow implies assistance rather than surveillance. WeTransfer could continue to collaborate. We needed to collaborate, but flow would help us define what role we played in the act of collaboration. Flow meant that we could maintain, and even celebrate, our lack of intrusion – because that particular lack, on all levels, was becoming more and more important to us.

This trait also fitted in with our exportable Dutch attributes. We aren't ever intrusive. Unlike apps and services that speak the language of flow and collaboration, but secretly monitor and record, our goal is to get and keep people in their flow, to leave them to themselves.

This way of positioning ourselves was becoming more and more important in the hiring process. Large tech companies can throw money at new hires, but these companies begin to contort and speak in opaque terms when new hires question them on data extraction and, generally, what they're using surveillance techniques for. We didn't have to twist ourselves to cover up our secret purposes. We didn't have to pretend to love and value the questionable practice of stalking individuals as they went about their online lives. The hiring process got easier.

And so did the product. By removing so many of the barriers, irritations and interruptions of the web, we created a tool that allows people to carry on doing what they do best.

With luck, this is just the start of a development process, enabling creativity without disrupting it. Developing products that genuinely aid and fuel ideation. Actually, I hate the word 'ideation'. Let's just say: We'll help you create.

Change was all around us. Our arrival date in LA was 1 August 2016, so we were in for geographical change, political change, and there was also an inevitable change in how we were perceived. There were some new lines in conversation we heard from our new American friends, sometimes repeatedly.

'Oh, so you're like YouSendIt!'

'Aren't you just like Dropbox but then with advertising?'

'So, you're a sort of *Vice* meets email?'

(Can you imagine such a thing? Shane Smith barking out: 'Hey, bro, you've got mail! *But I've got more mail!*' Gavin McInnes barking out . . . well, let's not imagine what he'd be barking out these days.)

There were some distinctions to make to our new American friends: We aren't Dropbox's cousin, nephew or niece. We don't act like them, talk like them or think like them. Don't get me wrong, we have huge respect for Drew Houston, but we have heard the 'funky Dutch cousin' statement many, many times and it makes us sound like a terrible house DJ.

Have you met Funky Dutch Cousin?

He will spin from 1 a.m. to 3 a.m.

And then there were the bigger questions about beliefs and company purpose. Maybe it was the horizons. Maybe it was all the time I spent in my car on those long drives in LA. Things started to become clearer when it came to who we were and where we were going. As someone from an advertising background, I was aware of the exposure we'd offered, giving away our full-screen visuals.

It never felt like a bad deal to give them away. Visuals weren't finite. By giving away our ad space it never felt, to me, like we were missing out or squandering some precious resource. We displayed the work of the best. Since 2009 we've given away more than 15 billion ad impressions to support artists and photographers. If you took our average price for this media, it would be roughly $22 per CPM (cost per thousand impressions).

When you look at it this way, we've given away over $330 million since our inception in 2009. A sceptic might say that we would never have been able to sell it all at that price, so let's halve it: $165 million to support the arts is still pretty good.

Last year alone we gifted 5 billion ad impressions. So we weren't doing nothing. We could always tell people we were doing our best.

The move to the US also meant we had faced another choice. Was it time for us to engage? What would that engagement look like in a world of responsible tech? Would it look stupid? Was it best to just keep our heads down?

In some ways, supporting artists was the easy choice, even artists who brought a political agenda to their work. Take the work of Giles Duley, a British portrait and documentary photographer who is known for his work documenting the impact of war. After losing both his legs and an arm after stepping on an IED in Afghanistan, Duley went on to document crisis and war, in time zones all over the world. He has worked with the UNHCR to document the ongoing refugee crisis. His work is formally beautiful and integral to our understanding of the world today. We helped Giles both design and build his platform Legacy of War and then helped him reach his Kickstarter goals and raise awareness.

You'd have to be heartless not to support Giles in his journey. It wasn't difficult for us. The photos were already done. We were just helping Giles on his way.

*

The next step for us would be getting involved in the making – introducing work, rather than just transferring it into the world. Companies were now intent on producing their own content. I was reminded of that each time I fired up Netflix. At the time, I was thinking a lot about the movement of the company. How does a company advance forward? We were definitely in motion, growing – and being led, in some cases, by the expectations of our younger staff.

Our decision to refrain from grabbing users' data and to build a business model that did not stress intrusion had become, increasingly, a political act. We were already making a statement by adhering to a lean data policy. People weren't hate-using our site. We had them, even for a moment. We were flowing with them, so to speak. (So Californian, I know.)

What could we do with this attention? It was as if we were, finally, conscious of our own growth. We were not just growing out of a panicky survival instinct. We weren't just plunging forward. There was increasingly something special, to me, about our transformation. From the act of transfer to – possibly – the act of creation.

Now, from the sunny shores of the Pacific, what were we going to create?

14: What to Do, What to Do

On 14 February, 2018, at Stoneman Douglas high school in Florida, seventeen children and teachers were shot dead. As a European in the US with kids attending middle school, this act of violence hit hard. We had just moved to the US. We were more than devastated. This was suddenly close. This was suddenly not just 'something that happened in the US'. Those classrooms looked like the classrooms my kids sat in every day.

It was senseless on so many levels; national, state and local. As a team, over dinner, with friends, I had many conversations about what we could do, what we should do – if we should do anything. My kids wrote letters to the government. We had just finished a 20-day festival in downtown LA called Into Action – an initiative trying to end the gun violence insanity.

One night I had dinner with some Dutch friends who were also living in LA. We discussed producing a film. While eating dinner, everyone talks about wanting to produce a film. It's an old LA custom. Again, in this small, persistent way, we thought our idea could be different. The film could raise awareness. It could also serve as an announcement of sorts, a statement of belief.

The following day, the producer Ellen Utrecht rang me to say that she had a director who was an ex-veteran, who was willing to shoot something within a week. The piece would feature veterans talking about the senseless nature of automatic weapons. She asked whether we would support it financially.

This wasn't exactly our country. This wasn't exactly our fight. But it seemed like the right step for us. I believed in the cause, obviously, but there was also a sense that it was time for the company to serve a different purpose. It was time for movement. This, for me, was part of the maturation of the company.

We performed a service well, and now that a platform had been created, this seemed to be how we should use the platform. Besides: Why not?

We hustled together the money. Ellen found the crew. My wife did the catering. The film was made and finished in a week: 38 million people saw that film, as it went viral on Twitter, pinned by Emma González, and was taken and broadcast at the March for Our Lives in Washington.

It went live alongside two other stories dedicated to examining the narrative of gun violence in the US. As a team we agreed to remove all advertising from the site, for the first time ever, and focus all of our efforts on gun reform over the weekend of the Washington march.

'Wow,' you're thinking. 'A company gets a conscience. A

Dutch company all of a sudden cares about the US.' But there was something else going on.

The second piece in the series was entitled *Anything But Guns*. It wasn't a film, nor was it a static piece of text. The piece was important because it pointed towards how WeTransfer could work with writers in the same creative way we'd collaborated with musicians and film-makers.

Anyone who has seen the state of the newspaper business will tell you, the future of print storytelling is up in the air. Who is able to tell stories these days? How can true stories be presented? There's great technology out there to combine with and complement text. But, again and again, we see the technology used in facile ways.

The tech, the design, the visual experience need to be paired with meaningful stories. With the *Anything But Guns* project, we applied storytelling lessons learned from Pixar and other animation studios. Narrative must be tested ruthlessly before technology becomes involved. There's a temptation to leap in, to make something first, to allow the technology to guide the story.

Anything But Guns allowed us to enter the realm of journalism. But it was a different kind of journalism. Just as animation sequences need to be written and rewritten, tested out, storyboarded, tested again, rewritten, our gun violence story was written and rewritten. The story took the form of an interview.

At first it looked like the reader was asking questions of an interviewee, a woman named Carolyn who lost her daughter in a mass shooting. But, again and again, the voice questioned the reader. Is it okay to go on?

Could Carolyn continue to tell her story? Could the reader handle the details? It was a choose-your-own-adventure where the narrative voice kept asking if the reader could handle the subject matter. During the experience, the reader was given multiple chances to opt out. The reader could just leave through exit points (leading to images of sun-swept beaches) if he or she couldn't fully deal with the story of gun violence and the attendant issues of grief. But the interviewee would always speak directly to the reader and offer reasons to stay.

A creative idea needs to prove itself. Increasingly, we're discovering what we can do as a company with our roots in design, with new technology and with editorial ideas. Facebook would like us to believe tech companies should be nothing more than platforms, passing information to people. They'd like us to believe that being a platform, absolving ourselves of responsibility, is something to aspire to. As part of a belief in responsible tech, companies have to begin to disagree. But what *should* we do with technology?

What impressed readers who came across the *Anything But Guns* project was the change that occurred over the course of the interview. A sense of intimacy grew between the voice onscreen and the reader. What interests me is the interchange of two prepositions: 'with' and 'in'. We realized that in our collaborations with readers we could draw them in. Increasingly, we can draw in readers. They can be 'with' a story and 'in' a story.

I don't mean role-playing, in that you dress up. More and more, I felt the company could not just transfer information but bring readers and collaborators and users – whatever you want to call them – closer to the story at the heart of it.

As storytellers we need to look at increasing the intimacy of storytelling, not pretending we are simply platforms. Whatever kind of narrative you're telling, whatever message you're trying to get across, we need to maintain contact in an increasingly fragmented world.

As I mentioned, the word 'flow' had become introduced at the company, and for good reason. How do you maintain that in a creative project? How do we forge a connection? First, people must trust you. Then, you must offer them something that warrants their trust.

With this piece, we saw we could lead readers through the story incrementally. That's why they stayed with the piece for ten or twenty minutes. It brought about a surprising closeness. Imagine a story – a tough story – where a voice is asking you if you're okay. Is it okay to go on? Would it be okay if I told you about the towel?

When the voice on the screen asks you, the reader, that question, you have the option to say yes. Or you can leave.

If you say yes, the narrator, Carolyn, goes on to tell you that, after her daughter died, when she could finally go into her bedroom, the toughest thing was not the belongings, the posters, the clothes, it was a towel in Kirsten's bathroom with two of her footprints still impressed in the fabric.

To be able to create a story, a program, that feels like a conversation with this person – a conversation that directs readers through a story, that challenges their expectations and draws them close – that's the kind of thing we saw we could create.

Great stories, tested for strength, and then brought into the world.

As the company grows in confidence, as we pivot out to build and collaborate and produce things, we know we have to pair our considerable technical skills with artists and creators. Don't monitor, don't mine them for data, but work alongside them. If we do this, we'll be able to handle whatever lies ahead – because in the coming years there will be issues to fight for and against.

Here is a case in point. In April 2018, in light of the impending changes to net neutrality in the US, we launched our own net-neutral internet. This comprised a free service to the local residents of Venice Beach, offering them simple, fast, snooping-free internet.

So where are we at now? The creative projects pushed us towards a long-term goal. When WeTransfer started, back in 2009, we were placing long bets that certain market conditions would move in our favour. We believed that 'small' data and transparency would build long-term trust. With the rise of fake news and the increased understanding (particularly in Europe) of data rights and privacy, punctuated by the introduction of the GDPR, market conditions shifted. Towards us.

Today, some 50 million people in over 195 countries use WeTransfer every month. Some basic settings have become de facto within WeTransfer, namely:

- *no sign-up*
- *a lean data policy/responsible tech policy*
- *30 per cent of media gifted to the arts.*

They're being adopted by others in an attempt to harness some of the trust that we have amassed over our short history. Not to mention that WeTransfer has a Net Promoter Score of around 80 per cent.

User experience, flow and frictionless movement across the site have been at the forefront of all decision making, with the priority being put on:

- *people first*
- *creativity second*
- *technology third.*

Over the last six years, we have given away billions of impressions. We've given them to friends, artists, illustrators, film-makers, charities and start-ups. If it wasn't a structured partnership, we never asked for anything in return.

This is important. To most people, WeTransfer is nearly invisible. We're just the transfer box – Bill Gates's 'plumbing of the internet'. The background belongs to someone else, but it accounts for 95 per cent of what people recognize as the brand. Therefore, curating and showcasing and working with other people and brands has always been, and will always be, important.

Today, when we highlight someone's work, we reach more than 80 million people per month. I'm proud to say that we now also have a home to provide more context to a lot of the artwork we feature; WePresent tells the stories of the artists who make the site so visually alive.

This push can make a huge difference to an up-and-coming

artist. From my perch, I love watching the process happen. It feels like we're using the reach of the internet for the right reasons. I get a kick out of seeing an artist grow and get somewhere – thanks, in part, to this exposure.

And the other thing I get a kick out of is making meaningful art ourselves.

15: The Glory of Not Being Told What to Do

At this stage, we get to feel something that is rare for a lot of tech companies: the glory of not being told what to do.

Is there any feeling more glorious? So there we were. Strangers in a strange land. We weren't implementing changes based on the insights we gleaned from data. As I have mentioned previously, we weren't a data-driven company. (Is it even safe to make that sort of admission these days? Or is it like admitting to a gambling addiction?)

At WeTransfer, we did what we thought made sense, and most of what made sense to us ran counter to the Bluffer's Guide to advertising online. Their message was everything we didn't want to do. And because it was our own money, because we weren't saddled with a rampant urge to transform ourselves into greedy, grasping Valley animals, we never ran out of funds.

If you start a business in the US and take money in the US, there will soon be someone at your shoulder, speaking in a charming American accent, telling you what to do. The advice they'll offer will always have worked in the past.

A glut of conferences out there in tech-land offer this same brand of tested advice. The purpose of the advice is to define the attributes of a successful software-as-a-service business. Many hold the key of how to dredge the most from your SaaS customers.

They're not lies. They're based on facts. But notice the past tense of 'based'. That word tells you nothing about the future.

We'd had enough of this cheap brand of TED Talk wisdom. It stirred in us a feeling related to one of Herman Melville's characters. Let's call it the Bartleby School of Business. 'We'd prefer not to.' Sure, you can TED Talk an idea until it has the veneer of truth. But we'd prefer not to listen.

Someone else could gather evidence and produce a shiny theory. We'd prefer not to believe. I've endlessly had Henry Ford quoted at me – until I later found out they weren't even Ford's words. 'If you asked people what they wanted before the automobile, they wanted a faster horse,' Ford *didn't* say. Every time I hear the quote, my eyes glaze over. It poses a bullshit punchline: 'They would never have asked for an automobile.'

Apple likes to employ this horsey mythology. Steve Jobs wasn't iterating some variation on existing computers. New ideas sprang from his forehead. People love that he shied away from doing fusty 'research'. Apple was based on his insight: 'You can't even imagine how different this next idea is going to be from a horse.'

It worked because, obviously – I'm looking up at you, St Steve – the guy was a genius. Geniuses, in Silicon Valley, are so much more enjoyable after the fact. In the present tense, no one enjoys considering a genius's brilliant advancements. Everyone wants the next step to be based on data.

System architects and data architects and data scientists – and a league of other surveillance miners – are always happy to tell you what you need to do, and which conditions need to be cultivated in order to succeed. They will know far better than anyone else. They are, after all, professionals. They've assumed the role in our society of high priests and priestesses.

Exceptions to the rule exist. I've noticed how much people love talking about a certain cadre of forward-pressing entre-preneurs, but they'd never dare follow the lead of these individuals. Everyone would love to be Elon Musk, but who would have dared follow him? And who would allow a Musk-y figure to be created now – in a dazzling burst of self-mythology – if he was playing with your own money?

This is probably why WeTransfer couldn't raise any. This is probably why we revelled in that glorious feeling of not being told what to do. We were told:

'That's not how you do online advertising.'

'No one's going to buy that.'

'File sharing is dead.'

'Gmail is going to kill you.'

'Google is going to kill you.'

'Everyone wants to destroy you.'

These were the messages emanating from the Valley: *YOU WILL BE DESTROYED.*

And this is the language: threats, hacks, destruction, burn. The stakes are high, environments turn toxic. If you can shield yourself from the *DESTRUCTION!!!* you might be able to usher a business into the world, especially if you're overseas, if you emerge from a more pliable environment, if you're not surrounded by other companies.

Our choices shielded the business from the violence associated with the language above. And, in our case, they shielded our users as well. Our freedom, our ability to forego being told what to do, allowed us to ignore fear-driven impulses all the way down.

The reason we had the confidence to keep the WeTransfer process open and transparent – instead of heeding the calls to install an awful sign-up form – originates, I truly believe, from the fact that Holland is so safe, you're not constantly alert to the prospect of a threat appearing.

Schools, for example, are not doing lockdown drills. Optimistic products come from optimistic environments. In the early stages, we didn't have to listen to a booming American voice telling us: 'The first person you need to hire is a security manager. The first hiring at WeTransfer has got to be somebody who can raise the firewalls, assemble the necessary protection and make sure the user understands compliance.'

Occasionally we'd consult an ethical hacker and then, after feeling misused and kind of dirtied by the experience, we'd agree to abstain from repeating that sort of encounter.

In the US, there are eleven bigger file-sharing services and they employ the same sort of unnerving language listed above. They talk about security, protection, and the various threats we face. We know that language. We speak the language. Of course we do. But our language is hidden. That's the part we hide. That's the part we take care of ourselves.

The difference between a design-driven business and a tech-driven business is that designers look for openness and simplicity. Technologists look for threats and weaknesses. A good designer aims to simplify, reduce clutter, focus and clarify navigation. A designer strives for cleanliness, simple signage and usability. Technologists are drawn inexorably towards features, add-ons, extensions, complexities beyond complexities, the production of better code, efficiencies. The driving force is to develop a powerful tool that will handle scale.

That's all fine and good. I'm not disparaging those goals. But somebody out there has got to Bartleby this: 'I'd just prefer not to go down that route.' Somebody out there has to be the beetle. Sorry: Beetle.

Like that Volkswagen car, WeTransfer has a classic design that we've just refined over time. The edges have become a little more rounded, but nothing has really changed. It's evolved. My hunch is that, in the future, we'll be considered a design classic. On the web.

And, to keep going with the Volkswagens, what we'll probably do in the future is explore what our Golf looks like, our Passat, but it will all come under the WeTransfer brand. Who's going to tell us otherwise?

Keep looking at some of the finest cars. No one is second-guessing the importance of a great engine. You wouldn't be able to start a car company without one. But don't minimize the importance of the designer building the exterior. The combination will rule the road – the well-tuned engine, small and efficient and clean, surrounded by, wrapped in, a design people will fall in love with.

(One differentiation: we don't compare ourselves with Volkswagen when it comes to trust. Got to be clear there.)

Yes, it all comes back to trust. Every single one of these transfers is an act of trust. It's an ongoing act of trust that this company's involved with, with countless millions of people around the world. Each one of those single actions has to be performed well. The file has to show up. You're transferring the stuff of life. It's worth letting people know that, so that they're aware of the stakes. So it doesn't sound like a utility service.

When we springboarded into the US, it was important our values didn't get damaged on the way over – for the sake of my kids and the company.

As a company, we were fully formed, out of our childhood. Thankfully, we had a strong set of values.

That was a good thing. We moved to the US two months before Donald Trump was elected. The world seemed younger then, fresher, more alive, in those autumn months of 2016. To move here and witness the election was to see a second Brexit on an epic scale. I suddenly felt less a part of an outwardly looking nation and more like an immigrant myself. Which I was.

Six months of disbelief followed, and a permeating sense of unease settled in. I'd moved my family to a country where they felt unsafe for the first time ever. In Holland, safety is taken for granted. Now we worried about everything, including basic human rights.

After the grim first six months, I realized this could be one of the most influential times to be in the US, both for my children and for my company. Both could actually be a part of some push to enact change.

What the move also stressed was that if you're going to be a company that allows for the free movement of data and ideas, take your ideas with you, along with your values. It's important to take the best values from different places. WeTransfer's service spans borders.

For instance, we could politely say no to the American idea of burning through. With some companies there's almost a touch of pride: 'We burned through forty million!'

There was a glory in saying no to this, too. Surely, there's got to be a way of celebrating frugality? If so, we haven't seen it in Silicon Valley.

Could it exist? Not when the goal is to change the world. Then you've got to be crazy. You've got to be able to go all out. Or was it all in, or go for broke, or the sky's the limit? Take another juicy selection from the smorgasbord of cliché. In the American context, frugality is ridiculous. How are you ever going to create massive change with frugality holding you back? Ask someone in Amsterdam and they might be comfortable telling you certain companies are not out there just to create massive change. They want to create something really good. Some of those companies with outsized global aspirations – aiming to be world changers – are just a little bit delusional, fuelled by the myths of Silicon Valley.

We had the glory of saying no to them.

If WeTransfer had started in the US, it would not be the company it is today. It's only 140 people – quite a lot when you need to stuff them in a minivan, but nothing compared to the hiring practices of the US. It's grounded. If you want a decision made, we'll decide it tomorrow and it will be done the day after.

If you've got a grounded Dutch company that is actually making sure the company stays real, you've got healthy checks and balances in place to go yeah, okay, that's good. We have a rule: we try to stay at 40 per cent EBITDA (earnings before interest and tax, etc.), so we want to stay profitable every year. We're not burning through cash for the sake of burning through cash.

Our goal is actually to have cash in the bank, to have a back-up plan, to make sure that we're going to be around in a few years' time. That's got to be one of the most boring concepts Silicon Valley will ever have encountered. What are you supposed to do? Use that money, go out and spend it, put it in something? Our viewpoint is, if we've got something really good that we think we're going to do, then we'll put the money into it. Until we do, we're going to keep it.

Put that into a searing TED Talk. 'How to Be Crushingly Responsible and Wildly Pragmatic. You Won't Believe Tip #5!'

That's our Dutch sensibility, exported to the sun of California. It also comes from the fact that, in the beginning, we didn't have any money. We were just desperately trying to put money in the bank to make sure that we could afford to pay the bills.

16: Responsible Business

For some reason we're still splitting our view of companies into two groups. We expect a fashion brand or an ice cream shop to exude a set of values to appeal to us and chime with our own. Yet we don't apply the same expectations to companies we think of as tech businesses. Somehow, different rules apply to them.

How fair is that, especially as the definition of 'tech company' changes? Conventional tech companies are no longer the only tech companies out there. Adidas and H&M are now in the same classification as Uber. There is no separation. You might guess where this is going: there should be no separation when it comes to the idea of being a 'good business'.

After all, values are more valuable than ever. In a recent survey by enso, the World Value Index, 78 per cent of millennials stated 'they were more likely to buy products from companies that shared their values', 59 per cent stated 'they felt able to affect the world around them' and 80 per cent said 'business can be a force for positive social and environmental change'.

When will companies listen?

Change starts with the founders, their value systems and the emphasis they choose to put on their contribution to society. Need an example? Here's one I came across the other day. T-shirt start-up Everpress could just manufacture, ship and finance garment merchandise for millennials everywhere. They could choose to ignore their responsibility to the environment, to the practice of manufacturing. They could take all the profits from a T-shirt campaign they do for the Great Ormond Street Children's Hospital. But they don't. They choose to donate the proceeds back to the hospital. They work hard to ensure products are ethically sourced. Their customers love them for it. This love translates into trust.

When will we get trust online as well as offline?

Step back from the internet for a second. Revel in its strange dualities.

Here is the most powerful educational tool of all time. Yet it's run by companies who don't want you to learn too much – at least, not about their own practices.

Here is a realm of connectivity and transparency – for some. But certainly not when it comes to how your data is being used by Google or Facebook.

Here are companies awash with the imagery of freedom, with talk of limitless exploration, boundary breaking, 'rebellion', 'punk rock', cutting of ties, cutting wires, cutting social constraints. All these freedoms can be yours – as long as you're bound with an unbreakable tie to the companies in powerful, secretive, ever-replenishing and shape-shifting ways embedded in their terms and conditions.

Here are companies in positions of power unlike anything we've ever seen before. But these positions come with dangerous vulnerabilities. There's vulnerability in their hypocrisy.

As we live longer and longer in the digital world and learn more, there will be a growing number who see past the obfuscation and begin to fashion their online lives accordingly. There will always be a frantic, shrill chorus from the incumbent powers, telling dissenters they're doing the wrong thing, that the status quo is natural. They'll offer new baubles: more 'free' storage space; more 'free' products; a lot more 'freedom' that isn't really freedom.

But it's precarious. It's all based on us accepting – and continuing to accept, ad infinitum – our new roles: endlessly used, endlessly drained, endlessly providing companies with our data, our natural resources, for free.

This is the point when the voice of Responsible Tech makes itself naggingly insistent. The thing about Responsible Tech is once you start thinking about it, it's tough to go back, or at least all the way back, to ignorance. Once the appeal of *not* working for anti-democratic monopolies sets in, hey, it feels pretty good. Once you start seeing a counter-internet forming in nooks and crannies, even in its current skeletal state, you'll begin to notice its presence.

It's tough to extricate yourself from the existing world of Facebook and Google. Of course it is. Recently, a study showed the average Facebook user had to be paid around $1,000 to agree to deactivate their account for a year. These habits have become part of the texture of our lives. How could a day possibly unfold without them? But this nagging idea, hatched and cultivated and growing, is exactly what Google and Facebook fear. Things could be different. We might, weirdly enough, think differently. It must pain employees at both companies to read the growing literature in which their places of work are portrayed as villains. It must pain the believers to think there is now dissent at the Googleplex.

It must be frustrating for companies set on denying and discrediting the past to find that ancient, dusty ideas can morph and change too – that regulation won't just die (or remain a European idea, like bidets). It must pain them when there's talk of anti-trust, a concept that is becoming newly relevant, reconfiguring, acquiring a new skin for this day and age.

Sure, there are academics bought off by Big Tech but there are now academics fired up and researching. There are computer scientists bought off by Big Tech but others researching. There are hackers bought off but others . . . you get the deal.

The same split is happening in the business world. Gaps are opening for companies, like ours, who will approach the future with a different attitude. Now is the time, the dawn, for the inadvertent pioneers. That's us. We're just a few folk from the design world. We didn't expect to pioneer anything, and I wouldn't lump us in with any of the truly great pioneers of history, or the internet (or even data transfer), but here we are. Inadvertently.

There are times I wonder how WeTransfer got to this stage, how this role opened up for us. Sure, we were born in a different country, we came from different backgrounds, we were denied money and all that comes with it. But we also decided against adopting a stance of us against them, us (the extractors) against them (the resource). There are others out there who think this way.

A company that has become an inadvertent pioneer should, at some point, try to issue an inadvertent manifesto when it comes to Responsible Tech. Ours would read:

we felt our way along
we trusted our instincts
we listened to the golden rule.

To us, Responsible Tech is not only respect for our customers, but respect for the world at large, respect for previous traditions and modes of interacting with others, respect for the beauty of privacy, of sanctuary, of core human values that can never be disrupted, trampled and scorned.

It's an acknowledgement that self-regulation often only helps the self-regulators. Respect – for people, for employees, for minorities, for whatever – also extends to respect for oversight. Responsible Tech, for us, means foregoing this ongoing trend in the me-me faux libertarianism tech world of what academic Shoshana Zuboff calls 'the systematic conflation of industry regulation with "tyranny" and "authoritarianism"'. Responsible Tech doesn't buy that. If you're moving so fast, breaking so much, maybe there's a consequence to the speed.

Responsible Tech is about behaviour but it's also about construction. For us, it's a way to examine the larger issue of what has been called 'extraction architecture'. Are we going to keep building this architecture at all costs?

It's a way of asking: Why do we keep building the invasive?

To my fellow tech workers, I say: Were these the great structures and systems you had in mind? Mining data sources such as how many times a person changes their battery, the number of incoming messages, how many miles travelled – surplus data? Is that what you dreamed about when you were studying and learning? Becoming a creep?

For us, Responsible Tech is a way to fact-check the term 'freedom' and bring to life a version of that word that companies who crow about 'freedom and connection' don't really want. Responsible Tech is the freedom of real rebellion, not Silicon Valley 'rebellion'. It's a new way of phrasing one of the oldest words: no. Responsible Tech salutes the English town that blocked the Google Maps cars from coming down their streets. *Why is this right?*

For us the phrase is a way of never letting behaviours that have been forced upon us by rapacious companies become normal – never letting them, as one commentator puts it, 'shade into normalcy'. Responsible Tech is a way of saying that we still choose what normalcy means to us.

Most tech companies follow inadvertent paths. Google, upon its founding, didn't set out to become the dredging, mining, superpower of surveillance capitalism. Facebook wasn't invented with intrusive scraping and Russian political interference in mind. If you're in this industry you'll know things shift: momentum shifts; ideas change; that thing you were dedicating 20 per cent of your mind to suddenly becomes the most important idea in the company. Compass bearings change. The territory you reach doesn't always resemble the map you unfurled at the beginning of the journey.

These days, it seems companies move in a single direction. They begin with optimism and good intent and inadvertently begin to resemble Skynet, only worse. Naive CEOs lose their naivety but continue expressing the same naive sentiments in public.

'I just want to connect everyone!'

'I just want to index the world's information!'

'I didn't mean it! Ruining the world, eroding privacy, turning every breath, every movement, every gesture into a commodity on the behavioural futures market? That was inadvertent!'

I'm no business mastermind, but from my vantage point I can see a trickle in the other direction. We didn't plan on becoming pioneers but we've inadvertently found ourselves in this position. We're inadvertently part of a movement, some weird and ragtag vanguard – one where we all look around and think: 'Are we doing this? Is this possible? In an age of scale and buy-outs and playing fields tilted in favour of the fast-moving, rule-trampling behemoths, is this actually going on?' It seems to be.

A divide is forming. Sometimes we can't quite plot the steps that took us here but we can see for certain that: a) There is a way to survive as a company in this vanguard, and b) We're not going back, we're not flipping sides, not after what we've seen. And also, let's ensure there's a c) Join us.

I put this call out to people who admire and appreciate all that tech has given us but know, from a gut instinct or on an intellectual level, that this endless invasive extraction is a new phenomenon in history and we've already ceded too much to internet giants with too little given back in return.

I put this call out to consumers who want to help and support the companies that choose to 'Ben-&-Jerry'. (Let's use it as a verb.)

I put this call out to the tech world and the developers and the engineers who might feel that on some level, personally or professionally, they've inadvertently drifted. They're working on stalking software. They're devising bits of extraction architecture that don't seem right.

Readers, be aware: these are intelligent people, drawn to tech for good reasons, and they're being used to make questionable tools. We all have to call on these people, appeal to them, especially those who seem to want to rebel and disrupt – at least with their music, their literature, their food sources, their spiritual practices, their political choices, their fashion sense, their choice of pet – but then they go to work for the most *man* version of 'The Man' yet, corporate beyond any powerful corporation's dreams.

People on the outside should know the tech world is full of 'rebels' and 'disrupters', some with really badass piercings and tattoos and personal styles and great music on their headphones, and there they are, at their desks, building the greatest tools of conformity ever devised. They might have loved reading *1984* but now, wow, they're truly doing Big Brother proud.

Readers should know that many of them feel they've inadvertently ended up in this position. I've met these people. They shake their heads and say: 'I didn't know how bad it was getting.' We've all got to invite them over to the other side of the divide. As long as Big Data gets bigger, so will the alternatives we hunger for – maybe never on the same scale, but they will continue to exist. So will the opportunities for those entrepreneurs who studied a little history, who can spot the new colours a monopoly might wear, or those creatives who value personal freedom and . . . well, let's just leave it there before the rhetoric soars a little too high and someone in the back reminds me my company just transfers files and shows full-screen ads. We're not exactly WeGandhi.

Scholars and writers mention the way the Big Tech companies capitalized on using our 'digital exhaust', the surplus of our interactions. As business people, let's also note another kind of surplus coming from the interactions we undertake online: anger.

We're only now starting to realize what's been inadvertently handed over, we're only just beginning to understand the shackles of terms and conditions. In the early 1900s, when there was a shift against the synthetic nitrogen fertilizers that were starting to become widespread, there was anger over what we were being asked to consume. No one could have imagined the pushback would transform itself into a multibillion-dollar industry. Will some form of Responsible Tech ever be worth that much? Who knows? We might need more education, more research, even more scandal before we reach that point of *Silent Spring*.

But we do know this: behaviour changes. It's happened before. We noticed that someone was messing with our intake. We were being pushed by corporate interests who wanted to get us to ingest more sugar, salt and fat. It went into us. The difference now is that we're talking extraction.

Now they want to extract our behaviour, our movement, our thoughts, the stuff of our lives. And suddenly, one day, some of us will decide that's not healthy. The next day, a few more people will decide the same. A consumer will look around for the companies offering something different. The first company they encounter, like WeTransfer, might say: 'Hey, we just decided we didn't need to know your data. We got big by accident.'

But the others, the next wave, will have a business plan. They might employ ex-insiders who have spotted weaknesses in the hulking edifices of the big companies. They may be riding the waves of an exposé or (another) scandal or even new regulation – opposed by the lobbyists of the existing superpowers but made law, regardless.

Look how the idea of the VPN (virtual private network) has moved, grown, become palatable, easy, necessary. Listen to what we're hearing now. Most importantly, pay attention to how your experience feels online – what is it like when you're hate-using Facebook? What is it like when you become aware of a queasy addiction to social media? When you read about what social media does to teenagers? How does it feel to know you're being mined, followed, tracked? How do you feel when you're clicking away your consent on a terms and conditions document you'll never read?

We don't need to get rid of it all. Not by a long shot. But we do need to change.

Think back to where we started – that stalking encounter in the shoe shop. Now look at the landscape. It's full of stalkers, hiding, watching, pretending to be good corporate citizens.

Right now, it often feels impossible to think of a different way. But we can build. We can support the new.

We're not gonna take this any more.

PART THREE
Asking the Questions

17: Examine

I knew from the beginning I'd have to consult the outside world. I knew there were no quick answers, and that I couldn't employ some surprise reveal at the end, which would point the way forward.

The best we can do is ask questions, and keep asking variations on those questions, keep reaching out to those who can provide their own particular truths at the time.

Throughout this book I've tried to bring together a range of views both from within and outside the tech world – I've captured just a small segment of the multitude of ways of thinking about the situation we're in. There's always room for more. Some people weren't as worried as I am about what's coming up. Some seem to inhabit their new digital selves with no hesitation, as if all will be well in the years to come. Some just do not care about the data collection I've outlined in these previous pages. For them, it's thrilling to be known in such a complete way.

With all these differing attitudes, we're hurtling towards the future. We're all going to have to grapple with it.

I've now been introduced to a few different survival tactics.

I've seen in bookstores 'fill this journal'-type books, and noticed in previous years the adult colouring book trend. This book has no blank pages or outlines of Mark Zuckerberg to fill in with pencil crayons, but I'd love for this final section to contain a grain of DIY spirit.

For instance, I was able to find a way to sit down with Stephen Fry. If you can do the same, I'd recommend the experience – for many reasons. But even if that's not possible – and please don't bombard his Twitter account with requests – there are individuals in your life who would like you to broach the subjects I've raised in this book.

These days, we need more conversation. There will be opportunities – even simply across age ranges – to ask people to outline their own views of where we're going. There are a million variations on fear out there; there are an equal number of reasons to feel confident. Each person brings a view of privacy, a standpoint on what's acceptable, a belief in what's right, a visceral reaction to these entities – Apple, Google, Facebook – that have come to define our lives. Some want change, some are irked, some are acquiescent, some glow with the fire of a new convert.

If there's one point to this book, it is this: examine.

Interrogate what's in front of you. Your questions will rarely be greeted with silence.

Ask a potential business partner: 'How do you want to confront issues of data collection and privacy?' It's a subject that's moving up from third date to first date material, and the great thing about taking on this bit of citizen journalism is that it leads to the heart of how people view themselves.

How should we be known? How much do you want to be known? Do we need to live in subservience to these Big Tech companies? How will you deal with the oncoming world of virtual reality? Could you ever take a trip without using Google Maps? Could I be part of your life without appearing on your Instagram?

Ask the questions. You'll be surprised at what you find.

Our relationships with machines are many things: sometimes cooperative, sometimes antagonistic. I had always wanted to talk to Garry Kasparov because he was one of the first – and he certainly won't be the last – to take on machines, head to head. Kasparov single-handedly defeated 32 chess computers in 1985, and then defeated Deep Thought in 1989. In 1997, he lost to the infamous Deep Blue – but only after beating it 4-2 in the previous year. Garry's understanding of AI is unparalleled. Combine this love of knowledge with his fiery political insight, and Garry's one of the most fascinating and opinionated people I've ever encountered. I wanted to speak to him about this intersection between the online and offline worlds, as well as social media, politics and AI.

Talking about data extraction always seemed like a good way to break the ice.

On the Fate of Other Countries and the Need for a New Vision
A Conversation with Garry Kasparov, Chess Grandmaster

Damian: Part of the issue that I see with Silicon Valley, and the way that the shift has moved to literally four companies that dominate the entire internet, is that the money associated with those companies and the VCs driving it are pushing them to continually have to search for better and smarter ways to extract data and to monetize the message or the news, whatever it is, whether it's fake or not. And so long as there's big money attached to it, surely there's that complexity.

Garry: That's a financial element of the story.

Because a lot of people, they are willing to buy fake news, they are willing to buy something that is contrarian, something that is sensational. Then these corporations that are basing their revenues and their fortune on advertising – and it means the number of clicks, the number of people who follow the certain items on their menu – then they have no incentives of fighting fake news. Moreover, unless they are pressured by the public through the political institutions, unless it happens, they will be just amplifiers of the fake news, and as a result in 2016, it could play quite a considerable role in deciding the future even of the greatest democracy on the planet.

People want new tools; they want maximum convenience. They want life to be turned into a flood of digital data, and then they complain about their privacy being infringed.

It's an interesting moment because it's the first time when technology is available to everybody. And people can basically enjoy the same services as those who are on the very top of the social pyramid. But the cost of that is that your information now, it's a part of the global network. And I think it's amazing people don't recognize that it's not a free lunch. The expectation from day one is that the internet is free, and it just brings us many good things.

Now, it is recognized that the price you pay is to download your data and basically to share your most intimate moments with, okay, maybe with a trusted source. Maybe with a corporation that can protect it. But at the end of the day, even if the company, say Google, is not violating your rights, then every company now is a subject for potential hacking. So technically you are investing your own personality. And you are at risk of being exposed.

That's a price to pay for many convenient things that make your life more exciting. And you have so many attractive options in front of you that you can reach out.

Again, it's an interesting psychological trade-off. A lot of people just haven't thought about it, and now we're at just the very beginning of this process of actually realizing that we are in the position to make these hard choices.

227

Because if we leave it to others, then we should stop complaining.

Damian: In Germany, it's a prominent conversation. Because they've always been very aware of the internet, they are well educated and wealthy. Whereas, I can imagine in other poorer countries they're grateful to get access to the internet and grateful for what it can bring in terms of education. They're far less critical of what is being given away.

Garry: Look, the problem is universal. It's a problem of relations between providers and data collectors and individual customers. The consequences are different. Obviously, in a developed world, there are ways of fighting back, there are ways of putting pressure on these big corporations. There are ways to protect individual freedom. But at the same time, people should realize that if they want Alexa at home, for their own convenience, for maximizing the effect of their time, of purchasing goods, they are sharing information with Amazon. And potentially with these others.

Damian: So how can an individual put pressure on a corporation then?

Garry: I believe that all these corporations, they are subject to political regulations and people who can vote, and by doing so they can change the government. The citizens in a free country, they have the means to create political conditions that will make it very costly for corporations to infringe their privacy.

Again, it doesn't mean that their data will be protected. But at least in Europe and America, citizens, they have an ability to constrain large corporations that are in charge of their data, to use it for their interests, to enhance their financial interest.

Now, as someone who was raised and born in a communist country, I'm really concerned about people who were not lucky to be born and raised in the free world. Because in China and Russia, in Iran and now in Turkey and in many other countries – actually, we're talking about 60 per cent of mankind – data being collected by state authorities will not just create problems for your consumer profile, it could sometimes even be a matter of life and death.

It's a serious moral challenge that while Apple, Google, Twitter and Facebook pretend – or at least they try to do their best to demonstrate – that they care about the protection of individual rights in the developed world, they willingly concede any data that is being demanded by dictators, just to protect their businesses in these countries.

Countries like India, I mean. Poor people – millions, hundreds of millions of them – who cares about privacy or security if there's free internet, and access to some of the services improves health and gives them a chance to sort of go ahead with their lives?

Damian: So what we're talking about really, at the moment, is the web as we know it. As we move into AI, as we start thinking about privacy and data and also ethics, how do you see the world moving around AI and how are we going to try and control some of that?

Garry: What's the difference? It's a new set of technologies, but it will not sort out all our problems – social, political, or economic problems. It offers opportunities. But unfortunately, you know, as every new technology, it offers opportunities for creation and destruction. Unfortunately, as every major technological breakthrough, it could be used for destroying, for a negative agenda, since it's easier. And at the end of the day it's still about people making decisions.

And the capacity for evil is uniquely human.

AI will be reflecting – as I said, the internet will be reflecting – our nature and our prejudices, and our beliefs. And it's, again, [a case of] while machines will know the odds . . . I don't believe they will be able to go beyond sort of calculating their decisions . . . based on odds that are, in turn, a part of the data that have been collected from human history.

Damian: Apparently, a third of US internet browsing has been done through private browsing. And apparently, there are 12.5 million people in the US that use VPN for private use. So let's play this forward, that people are using VPN, they're using private browsing, and we're no longer able to target advertising, and advertising is no longer the future of the monetization of the web.

Any thoughts on what the future of the monetization of the web might look like?

Garry: I'm a great believer in the invisible hand of the markets, you know? I think if technology is in great demand, there will be a way to pay for that, and again, if Google doesn't manage to adjust to new realities, there will be another Google.

Damian: Who is in control?

The perception of the man on the street is that Google, Facebook, Apple and Amazon are in control. However, they're only in control so long as we'll allow them to be, and we as consumers totally determine whether or not their business exists. We could collectively change their business tomorrow.

Garry: But we go back to the same issue: people want convenience.

They want new tools. If you have something better on the market, they'll buy it, but you need something truly revolutionary to appear, which I doubt very much can happen since these corporations, they are quite good, not at inventing new things, but at buying any potential inventions and killing them if they could threaten their business model.

*

Garry: We have to come up with a new vision. That's why I'm also interested in just asking the same questions, but probably in a broader sense. So what would you expect from this great technology? Say, how soon we will walk in the red dust of Mars? Not for the sake of actually having a great movie, or just another bunch of tweets coming from the first crew, or from the president who authorized this flight. But to restart the process of exploration. To make sure that we will bring back risk as a factor in our lives. We will not be, we will no longer be afraid of taking risky endeavours, and we will actually recognize that risk is a necessary part of any profitable business.

Damian: Elon Musk is clearly not afraid of risk.

Garry: I'm in awe with what he's doing, but it's not about one individual, it's about the drive of society. One of the most quoted phrases from inaugural speeches, most likely, comes from 1961, JFK's, 'Ask not what your country can do for you.' And now, can you imagine a politician today asking this question?

How long will he or she survive? By basically telling people that they're responsible for their own future, they're responsible for the well-being of their country. Or coming from the same speaker, JFK, the moon speech. So, we're going to land on the moon and do the other things in the next decade, not because it's easy but because it's hard. Again, can you imagine any politician today rallying people behind something which is hard, not easy?

It's very important that we recover this spirit, because that's the only way to fix things. It's a big picture issue, and that's what I'm interested in. It's not about something being broken and [needing] to be fixed, in one compart-ment or another. It's, I think, about trying to compartmentalize things, to sort of micromanage them. We're losing the big picture, the vision of the future.

Again, I wish more people will recognize that we have to expand. Physical expansion was always a very import-ant, if not the crucial factor, of human progress.

It's horizontal versus vertical development.

And we are staying horizontal for a long time.

• • •

Sarah Drinkwater moved from Google to the Omidyar Net-work, the firm created by billionaire Pierre Omidyar, to continue her work with communities and to really try to test and scale interventions that help maximize the tech industry's positive contributions to a healthy society.

Omidyar Network is one of the very few investment firms that are looking at sustainable investments. 'We seek to create a more equitable economy, promote responsible technology that improves lives, expand human capability, and discover the emergent issues that will shape our future.' Who would ever have imagined this statement would be on the home page of a venture capitalist firm?

A Conversation with Sarah Drinkwater
Director at the Tech and Society Solutions Lab,
Omidyar Network

Sarah: What's so interesting about Omidyar is we're investing for profit and grant making from the same pot of
monies. It's the same fund.

We were founded in 2004 with this really cool belief:
technology being a force for good. At the time, we were
imbuing the notion of tech itself with certain values that
we presumed to be across the board.

I think it's become obvious that was perhaps naive of us
in 2004.

Look at tech now. It is very clearly a tool. And it's
very clearly imbued with the values of the person that's
created it.

So the metrics that we assign to the investments we
make are really untraditional. We're looking at positive
impact on the overall scene. When we're looking at
growth, it's traditional and atypical.

We have the freedom to do that partly because
we have one funder. If I were based in a very different
fund, we'd have a certain number of stakeholders to
please.

That's why having one fund can be powerful. As
long as that person agrees with the mission you're working on. It helps you to work in a way that is more positive,
I think.

Damian: Omidyar has this thesis of investments in positive returns, right?

Sarah: Positive returns is broader than just money, if that makes sense. It's broader than just a financial goal. So when we talk about our impact report, when we talk about positive returns, it's partly financial, but the return is a small part of that.

We're far more interested in overall system change. So when we're looking at things like financial inclusion, how do we change systems in an entire scene? Visual ID. How do we drive adoption of digital ID across West African countries, for example.

It's this unusual space between social impact and traditional VC. And that's what really appealed to me as a person when I recently joined this team.

Damian: It appears to me to be a million miles away from Google. When you're talking about a company that has best intentions, or that's looking for positive returns, did you see any of that in Google?

Sarah: I was really insulated in some ways.

The field that I've always worked in is community.

The last ten years of my career has been around pulling people together – in a way that is making sense of big cities, making sense of the internet, making sense of this distraction economy where everyone's trying to get your attention the entire time, but there's no real value in it.

This goes back to Instagram. Instagram is full of people who want to show stuff that you can buy or experiences you're not having right now.

So I joined Google. I was hired by them to run a community on Google Maps. I worked on an engineering team I loved. It was really, really, really far away from making money.

The last four years, I was running a physical space. I had this really unusual experience. It was quite naive in some ways. I experienced the best part of Google.

In the last year, all of these things began appearing in the press that made me pause and question where I was working. I was running a space of entrepreneurs, it was free, it was open access. It lived a lot of values that I have: it was global, diverse, it was helping people start companies.

I believe in that notion of micro-entrepreneurship and growing in a way that's right for you.

In the last year, I kept thinking: I'm pro-business, but I don't think of business as being pure – 'make money at all costs'. I believe in this notion of business being a powerful force for good change in communities.

That was the driver behind my move into the Omidyar Network. When I was thinking about leaving Google, I began looking for opportunities elsewhere, and a lot of traditional VCs really didn't appeal at all.

The reason why this particular role was interesting was, okay, I believe in better business, but I also believe that traditional tech must change – whether it's classic 'VC baking better ethical decisions into the decisions they take when they invest in the company', or whether it's starting out with the right process.

When you guys began WeTransfer, it was just part of your ethos. It was who you were as people.

The challenge that we have is that it's just not on the horizon for a lot of tech founders. That's because they are too similar as a group. They're based in very particular parts of the world.

How do I take what I liked about Google – the openness, the transparency? People there generally are really nice and really kind. How do you take that, but leave behind a lot of the naivety about what you're actually building at heart?

Damian: Within a company like Google, do you think it's fair to assume best intent?

Sarah: I guess my experience has always been that you lead with trust – whether it's in your personal relationships, or whether it's in your work relationships, or whether you're building a team. That's the only way that you can build something strong for the long term. And that's the only way to live, I think.

What's interesting about Google, at this point in time, is I think they have the mindset they're still a very small company. And they're not. They're a massive company with incredible, incredible influence in many, many, many areas of life.

When they began, tech was its own thing in the corner. It was a silo. And tech now: it's government, it's shopping, it's democracy. It's all of these things that it wasn't ten years ago. A lot of the leaders have been with them since the early days. They've been working in classic tech for ten, fifteen years. Part of the reason why you guys are different is you're not from classic tech backgrounds. If I'm right in thinking, a lot of your founders are designers or have a design background.

And this is partly the reason why you see Zuckerberg being shocked and surprised, again and again and again, about the influence of his platform – in a way that, to me, feels a bit disingenuous sometimes. It's a little bit like, don't be ridiculous. Of course you have this power. But it's almost as if, in his mind, he's still got this small company that is doing one very particular thing, with this altruistic mission to connect the world.

With Google it's the same thing. I saw a lot of really, really, really, really good intent up close. I didn't have experiences working with people who genuinely did things for the wrong reason. And that's why, when press stories would come out about Project Maven, for example, it was horrible, as somebody who worked there.

That's why it's so hard for those companies to change. They're not challenged enough internally. They're not humble enough, I would say, about who they are in the world. They have these grand intentions and these grand ambitions.

I particularly point to the way Silicon Valley looks at

European regulation. I definitely saw a lot of, 'Oh, well, in Europe it's all about regulation. It's all about politics.' That felt patronizing. When actually, increasingly, with tech being so borderless, I'm personally pro-regulation. There's a lot of positive regulation out there. I love what Alexandria Ocasio-Cortez versus ASC is doing around tax reform in the US Congress, for example. These ideas that could be seen as quite radical, six months ago, are now quite mainstream. I love the Overton window shifting on that kind of thing.

It's really interesting to analyse setting up the version of the first phase of any company. Are you a B Corp? How do you think through setting up in the right way? Because the minute you're off to the races, it's too late a lot of the time. There's a lot of good intent out there, but increasingly, to a point, the structures that we live in make it really, really, really hard.

I'm excited about companies that don't take VC funding. I'm excited about companies that start small and are revenue positive to start with. I'm excited about companies that put themselves out of that whole system to start with.

It seems to me that that's the only way you can grow differently.

Damian: In Holland, it's really difficult to raise money. So it's more common that people will bootstrap. You have much more control over your business.

Sarah: It's also good that it is harder to raise money.

Damian: It was the greatest pain point for us at the time, but in hindsight it was the best move, because we were able to keep the values that we had. As soon as you've got forty million in the bank, everything changes.

Sarah: And then you have the pressure of spending the money as well.

If I think back to my last start-up, we didn't know any better. We were very naive. You do stupid things when you're naive. And one of the worst things that could have happened to us is somebody saying yes – in terms of money.

We're in a very different world now, where founders that I respect are choosing to go it alone. If you are in the fortunate position that you guys were in – 2009 or whatever – of nobody saying yes, that is the really great thing in the long term.

Damian: What's it going to take for VCs to change and to look at businesses that are perhaps values-driven, or responsible data, or much more trust orientated. Is it possible? Can VCs do that?

Sarah: I'm an optimist. I think things are possible. But I guess, if you think about trust, we're living in this quite sort of trust-deficient world, where we don't really trust in government, we don't really trust each other.

With the model of VCs, it's all about people. And there are people who work as VCs that I like an awful lot, that are trying to be different, that are working on very different models. I'm thinking of people like Indie.vc, et cetera.

In this world where share prices are going down, economic growth is slowing, it is really hard for VCs, because they're ultimately responsible to their investors, the partners, et cetera.

Conversely, it makes it harder for VCs to experiment. It makes it easier for small companies to be experimental themselves. We've been searching for the last ten years for the next Google, the next this, the next that. I think we've all realized now that a lot of those companies came from a particular moment in time, and we might not see them again. That's not a bad thing.

I'm interested in sustainable growth, and VC money that is appropriate in terms of scale that gives you more than just the money, that gives you that real support, the opening of doors, the network effect that you're looking for.

There are funds working in that space that are quite interesting. Not enough right now, but I think there are increasingly experiments that are happening in that space.

Will it come out of Silicon Valley? I don't know. I personally suspect not, and that's partly just my cynicism about the Valley as a whole, which is even funnier now that I'm moving there.

Damian: I was going to say.

Sarah: Europe gets overlooked the entire time in terms of this space. Toronto has loads of really interesting work in this space. So does New York. So does London, I would argue, but that's because I'm a biased Londoner.

Damian: Will consumers lead the change?

Sarah: They have, in some ways. Certainly not with massive companies. If you look at campaigns like DeleteUber, they don't really matter to Uber, if that makes sense.

They cause a splash on social media, they get written about in the papers. You read about it in *The Economist*, for example, but it's not enough. It doesn't drive real change, I would argue. I can't imagine that Uber is sitting at their desks worrying about that – certainly not somewhere like London, where there are no real competitors.

We're still using those products. We use them and we hate them in the same way that I still have Facebook, but I hate it. I still have Uber, but I feel bad about it. It just leads to consumer guilt and shame, and that's not good.

If I think about how good I feel using products like Glitch, how bad I feel using products like Uber, that's a really strong comparison of how I as a consumer feel using those different things.

You want your brand to be loved, right? Not used under sufferance.

Consumers can help, but I don't think it's enough, ultimately, while you're making money. If you look at

Facebook in the last year and the incredible decrease in stats, I still think it will take a lot more for them to change what they're doing.

Damian: But is it down to Facebook to change it?

Sarah: No. I think that's a really interesting question because I think one thing Rachel [Doteveryone] and I talked about a lot is it doesn't take one group alone. It takes industry plus government plus citizens. It takes all of us as a group to say this must change, this must be better.

But while those groups want and need such different things, while government is so bad at designing tech itself, it's hard for them to be leading it.

And particularly with the UK and the US, you've got Brexit as a distraction, you've got Trump as a distraction. You've got the hyperbole of the press. I think a lot of the media coverage has been not as rational as I'd like it to be.

Industry itself is not there strongly enough.

There's a really interesting moment where we need change. It's not really clear yet where it will come from. We're seeing pockets of positivity, bits of good behaviour and pockets of good stuff.

Our work has been very cross-functional in that way. We decided that one challenge was this problem is too big to be solved by any one group individually. We had to find a way to convene quite different actors, if that makes sense.

We've not done a lot with policy makers, but we have been speaking to them. We've done quite a lot with product teams at large and mid-sized companies.

There are companies that we think do great work: you guys are one. I think Stripe are doing really interesting work. That's part of the reason why we've worked with pockets of good industry, if that makes sense. For example, Responsible Computer Science Challenge, the letter for that was signed by investors, funders, founders, product leads, government people like Nicole Wong, for example, who are thought leaders in that space.

That's part of the reason why we've really tried to have that approach of working across systems in the same way that everyone does too, I guess. Having that approach of community building, which again is my great passion.

How do we build shared trust even though we have different takes on different things? How do you build a movement in that way?

Damian: Where would you like it to go? What do you think it could be like?

Sarah: We're at a really interesting inflection point.

I grew up with tech. My dad has worked in cybersecurity and military systems really since the seventies, and we have lots of debates around this. My dad is highly ethical, a kind of old-school developer, if that makes sense. He calls Apple 'Macintosh', has massive problems with

Google and Amazon, which is why it's so funny two of his kids work there.

Have worked there, I should say.

His approach was always that a lot of the systems we use now were developed by the military in a way that had to be highly regulated and highly thoughtful.

I'm kind of a pacifist. I'm quite anti-military as a person. He always said the reason it was so good that DARPA funded the original internet was because it had very clear constraints, because it was developed for military systems.

The military had to be incredibly thoughtful in how they were developing things. I think we forget the origins of the internet a lot of the time. We think of the internet as Facebook, we think of the internet as XYZ, we think it's a noughties phenomenon. It really is not. It's decades old. Centuries, in many cases, for things like algorithms and stuff. Charles Babbage and all that kind of thing.

In the future, we'll hopefully have a clearer understanding that technology is all around us. It's embedded in everything that we're using, whether it's our tube pass in London, whether it's CCTV as we walk around the streets. I hope that as individuals we'll have an increased understanding of the kind of world we want to live in.

If you look at Chinese value systems and Russian value systems of the internet, they are very different to the world I want – as a European and as a person.

I hope that, in the future, we have more individual control, but also that we have an understanding as a group and a community of what technology is for.

With my interest in building communities, I see the internet as a bit like a hammer, right. You can use it to build a house or use it to smash things up.

Where I believe tech is used most powerfully is where it's helped me make new friends, it's helped me keep in touch with my husband when I've been away from home. It's helped me have new experiences, and it's driven me offline quite fast.

That's where it's really powerful. The internet that loops you, that keeps you online the entire time, it's not a good thing. The internet that discriminates is not a good thing.

People talk about humane tech, and I don't love that because ultimately everything we do is humane. We're humans. But I mean the humanity of tech, if that makes sense: taking decisions thoughtfully, being offline more than online, being communal rather than individual.

What is difficult is much of this rests on us dismantling capitalism, which is my personal hope. That's really hard to do, because we live in it, right? But I guess my hope would be that we have continued debates around this, that we have companies that we hold up as beacons of hope, like yours, who are doing cool shit, and we keep asking the right questions, particularly for Omidyar, for us as a team. Keep challenging, keep bring-ing the right people together, keep testing possible solutions, and hopefully striving towards answers, I guess.

Damian: Your family Christmas dining table is an example of how we need to progress. You, your brother or sister at Amazon, and your father, who despises both. On the internet we're living in an echo chamber. The future needs to be more of a debate club.

Sarah: That's really interesting.
The first time my husband, who also works in the internet, came home, he was so terrified because his family don't talk about tough things. That's all we talk about as a family. That's all we debate.

•••

Not only does he bear an uncanny resemblance to Jeff Bridges, Peter Thum is a master of holding the silent pause. But when he does speak, he's an eloquent person who can be relied upon to discuss another of the strands I'm interested in exploring. How do we act with responsibility within our current framework? We can't change everything, right now. Thum founded Ethos Water back in 2005. He later sold the company to Starbucks. Since then he has also co-founded Fonderie 47, an organization that takes assault rifles from war zones and turns them into jewellery, and Liberty United, which takes illegal guns from US cities and turns them into jewellery. The proceeds from both ventures fund programmes to reduce gun violence.

A Conversation with Peter Thum
Entrepreneur and Investor, Founder of Ethos Water

Peter: My mom was a teacher, and my dad was a surgeon.
They were very involved in the community where we
lived. They were very involved in the church that I was
raised attending. It was clear what their values were. Not
necessarily by talking about them, but by demonstrating
them: you live in a place, and you're part of a community,
and you look out for your neighbours, and you look out
for people who maybe aren't necessarily your neighbours,
through the way that you live your life and the work that
you do on a daily basis.

Those values are part of what led me to come up with
Ethos Water.

When I was graduating from college, instead of taking
one of the jobs that I was offered, I moved to Berlin. I
thought it would be very interesting to live and work in a
place where the world was changing so rapidly, rather
than reading about it in the newspaper. After several years
of working in Germany, I went off to business school, and
then I joined McKinsey & Company, because it seemed
the best place to learn, at a high level, across functions
and issues.

Because I had previously worked in the wine industry,
one of the assignments I got was to work on the merger of
two wineries in South Africa. I ended up working and
living in South Africa for about half a year. As I travelled

around the country doing my work on the project, I spent a lot of time around people who were very poor. On the other hand, the client employees were comparatively very wealthy.

Water was one of the big problems I saw first-hand.

I left South Africa thinking that this is a problem that affects hundreds of millions of people – about 1.2 billion people at the time. I wanted to try to do something about it, but didn't really have any specific idea what I could do.

The next McKinsey project that I was assigned to involved helping a soft drink manufacturer with profitability. During the project, I realized that bottled water was not only a growing business, but also a business where there were a set of brands that sold themselves to consumers based on origin and fancy packaging.

It occurred to me that I could create a competitor brand where the emotional benefit wasn't that the water came from some remote place where it was supposed to be pristine and better, but rather the benefit was that when you buy a bottle of water, that bottle, that purchase, is funding water access for somebody in need, in a place in the world where clean water access is not available.

That idea became a plan. The plan became Ethos Water while I was still working at McKinsey. I left McKinsey, and the UK, to come home to the US, which at the time seemed like the only place that had a big enough market for a brand idea like Ethos Water. I understood the UK wasn't going to be a large enough market, and that the structure of the trade there wasn't going to be favourable enough. Long story short: after trying to start it as a not-for-profit organization, Ethos Water became a business, we raised some money at the TED conference, and then were acquired by Starbucks.

But the really interesting thing is that Ethos started as an idea to try to address the problem: a mission with a business. It didn't start as a business that was modulated after the fact by the value system of its owner.

In this way, it was more like Paul Newman's business than it was like Ben & Jerry's.

Ben & Jerry's was an ice cream shop that was filtered through the value system of its two founders. They made business decisions in their supply chain, and in the charitable giving of the company, that were about who they were, as people, not about what they were trying to accomplish by creating a company.

Ethos existed *only* because of its mission. I never would have started that business had I not believed that the intersection between this huge issue and the burgeoning bottled water business provided an opportunity to potentially create dissonance in the problem.

A fundamental core purpose at the centre of a business, which drives strategic decision making for that business, and positioning over time, is critical for that business to be able to answer these kinds of fundamental entity questions about pursuing purpose over time.

One of the reasons why technology companies struggle

with this is because, in a culture that's dominated by engineers and Darwinian product focus, there really isn't a lot of consideration given to what they're going to stand for.

Ethos has been an interesting case because it's a single-purpose brand, and it has one product that stands for one thing. That message – helping children get clean water – has a lot of leverage.

Ethos was acquired by Starbucks in 2005. It is their bottled water brand in all of North America, certainly in the US and Canada.

Damian: Were there any other benefits from focusing on water?

Peter: Yeah. I had intended to create multiple products under one brand and filed for trademarks under multiple categories. Bottled water for Ethos was a lot like books for Amazon. The reason that Bezos started with books was because they were easy to ship, there was a big catalogue, people wanted books, they would appreciate the ability to get a book shipped to them that they were interested in. There are a host of reasons why books were good, but they were also a good starting point upon which you could build the rest of the business.

The question is whether or not large companies can create businesses like Ethos or Ben & Jerry's, without the values that the founders started with.

I don't know that it is impossible, but I think it's very

hard, because the people involved are driven by traditional views of business strategy, economics and shareholder value. Their careers are shaped by this culture, and markets still are dominated by these ways of thinking.

In addition, social purpose is very difficult to retrofit on to a business – whether it is a small company or a large, publicly traded company – that has been built and financed with this traditional set of lenses. Here's an example from my own experience of the possibilities and the limitations of social impact. When Starbucks was looking at buying Ethos, Pepsi – which had a joint venture with Starbucks – heard about it. They came up with a competitive brand concept. They basically said: 'Here, we can do this too. You don't need this Ethos brand. And you don't have to donate as much money to the cause.' At the time, Starbucks was an $8 billion company that was growing rapidly, and they had a joint venture with Pepsi, a $35 billion company, to make and market beverages. In this context, the decision to go with Ethos Water was unorthodox to say the least, but it paid off.

Following the acquisition, I said to the Starbucks team: 'Look, we should donate ten cents per bottle sold. You're going to be able to increase the donation by this much, but you also should increase the price to the consumer more than you are planning to do.' But they didn't want to increase the price to the consumer the way that I was suggesting, because it would have increased the total basket price of the average Starbucks consumer purchase for anyone buying bottled water, in addition to other products, above a threshold that they did not want to cross.

They had more to take into consideration than just my wants as the guy who was running their water brand.

But they later told me about the economics of the Pepsi proposal. Pepsi was proposing giving something like half a penny per bottle, or something like that – some ridiculously small amount of money in comparison with our plan.

But Starbucks made the choice to go with Ethos Water and then they enabled us to give more than two and a half times more money per unit sold than we were able to do as a stand-alone company. Then they agreed to a public commitment to donate $5 million to projects over the next several years, which was not trivial and required approval from the CFO and the board.

Ultimately, over time, I realized that all large companies view the financial aspect of the social mission as a cost.

The people who run big companies are, as individuals, not generally rewarded in their careers for leading with social purpose or for taking risks. Understandably, they make career and business choices that are primarily about competing for positions and influence rather than about creating things or considering social impact.

Damian: When you started Ethos, did you raise money, or did you start it before raising money?

Peter: I started it before raising money.

Damian: Do you think you could have started it raising money?

Peter: I tried.

Damian: The people that make up the VC world are in control of a lot of tech destiny. They're basically deciding whether or not something is going to be made or broken. The thing that we're seeing today is a lot of tech companies want to be bootstrapped. They don't want to take VC money because of the fact that those VCs are often dressed in the same blue shirts, khakis, Patagonia jackets. They look the same, think the same, decide the same things for everybody, using calculations based on the past to determine the future.

With WeTransfer, we couldn't raise money in the beginning, because we didn't fit the mould.

Peter: I have a friend who's a former McKinsey guy, former bank guy, former VC. He's had a lot of business lives, and he recently said: 'If you can't raise friends and family money, you don't deserve to get VC money.' And I said: 'I understand what you're saying, and that sounds really pithy, but that's wrong.' There are companies that should raise no outside money. There are companies that should raise only friends and family money, and there are some companies that should only raise VC money. If you are starting the latter type of company and the capital is available and you need to go fast then don't go get friends and family money, just go get the VC money, because your business is probably intended to get bought in a trade sale after rapid growth in a rapidly changing market. Of course, these statements might all be different in a recession when the pool of VC capital that is available shrinks dramatically.

There are people who see things, about the way that they think they can create something, or the way that the world could be, the future could be, and no one in their right mind would give them any money. And they'll still make it happen.

And for those people, financing isn't even really a question. They don't give a shit about the money. They're going to do it anyway. It's going be uncomfortable to not have money, but that's not going to stop them.

They would be the wrong people to be the founders of something that's purely about creating a component to be added to Google.

When you started WeTransfer, you didn't really exactly know what was going to happen. Right?

Damian: No, no we didn't.

The majority say that when they started a business that becomes successful, that they just knew from day one that it was gonna work out.

How much of that is true?

Maybe you have an idea that, in some way, shape or

form, you believe in yourself that you can pull something off, you can make it happen. But actually, the thing that ends up being a success, is that the thing that you really bet on in the beginning, or is it 20 per cent of the original concept that you have?

Certainly that's the case with WeTransfer.

There was something in it, but the lever that worked the best wasn't the lever that we thought was going to be the business. It was nice to have.

Peter: If you brought together a group of people who didn't know each other to create WeTransfer, do you think it would have succeeded?

Damian: No.

Pretty much everybody that joined has tried to erode, at some point in time, the key factors that are the biggest success at WeTransfer today.

And that leads to the following. At a certain point, people would say: 'You've got a great brand, it's doing really well. Why don't you drop that ten cents to three? Why don't you just sell it as water, and forget about all the other complicated bits?'

Peter: Absolutely.

It's this idea of purpose. At those times you don't necessarily have to double down, but you have to ask yourself: 'Why am I doing this?'

If you're pursuing social purpose in a way that you can

modify the mission, should you be running a company that has the mission at all, anyway?

If some percentage of the top line is being used for the purpose of accomplishing a social mission, then . . .

Maybe I can put it another way. I've had people come to me and say: 'I'm starting a company that's gonna do X. How can I incorporate social mission?' My advice is usually: 'Don't even try to do it.'

Damian: I hear that a lot too.

Peter: 'Don't waste your money.'

Damian: If it's not the core foundation of the house, if it's not the core foundation of the building, someone comes along and knocks it down, because they think it's ugly, or it doesn't fit, and it doesn't quite match, and it needs to be amended. That will be almost guaranteed to happen.

You've chosen to start a company that's got a very strong mission.

I believe it's the right thing to do today, whatever industry you're in.

We should be operating and thinking like that. And I think the market is looking for more people who start companies thinking in such a way.

I see it being a bigger part of the employment and recruitment process going forward. Graduates will be much more selective, looking for those values, rather than travel allowance or whatever it was that I was looking for when I graduated, looking to be working in a consultancy.

Peter: Do you find they're looking for jobs at companies that have mission at the core of their founding?

Or do you think that they're looking for companies that have the essence of missions sprinkled around their office?

Damian: I can't speak for everybody.

The ones who are critical thinkers, better educated, more questioning when coming into a company, want to find out what the diversity policy is. What is the ethnic diversity split amongst employees? What does the company do in terms of giving back? What role can they play in serving the local community?

We hear those sorts of things a lot more – one of the reasons that people come to work for WeTransfer, to be frank, for less money than most other companies in tech. Not because of the aspiration to build and work with the best engineers, but mostly because of the aspiration to work in a company that does good, in some shape or form.

Peter: Your employees are choosing to come to belong somewhere, and be a part of something, because of the way that the company impacts the world. And your company is capitalized differently, probably has a different ability to incentivize those people, both in terms of pay and equity: future equity, exit options, things like that.

Most people in a publicly traded company would look

at that the same way that they look at Ethos giving away a nickel, as being a cost problem.

To me, it's just a positioning choice.

Damian: And it's a risk. The differentiator we have in the marketplace enables us to employ people that will be considering us against a company like Dropbox, and choose us over them, even for less money, and less equity, because of the values that we have.

When you're talking about 'mission', anybody that you speak to in the VC world treats you differently. I don't know if you've had that experience, but certainly, in a room of VCs and tech entrepreneurs, there is a very clear line as to which side of the room I sit on, and which side of the room the guys with the money sit on.

It takes a long time for that line to blur, for those traditional VCs or traditional business people to understand the difference, and actually to see the potential in a company like ours. It's really fascinating to watch. Have you had the same experience?

Peter: Somewhat, but in a different way. I've never sought capital from any of those people, so I haven't had to be in conversations where I have to deal with the fact that they're going to judge me.

They may be judging me, but they're not judging me based on the way that they think the business world should work. But I have had conversations with guys like that, and we sort of agree that we don't necessarily think that there's anything wrong with the way that the other person thinks about the world.

We just don't necessarily think that the way that they think about the world is necessarily right.

•••

Was there a more interesting approach to the state of the internet? Was there a way to smuggle in more values? Aaron Koblin is known for his data visualization. As the founder and CTO of virtual reality company Within, he's thinking deeply about the future of VR, which will be upon us sooner than expected. My conversation with Aaron led me to return to some of my old questions: How can trust and empathy exist online as we migrate to these new forms?

If we can make the internet a better place, what does that better place look like, and how do we get there? Whatever you think of it, VR will play a crucial role in where we're going. What's the best way to integrate it? Will it help with flow? Or will it just be a way to gather more data?

On Empathy, Flow and VR
A Conversation with Aaron Koblin, digital media artist and entrepreneur

Damian: With VR there are some capabilities and attributes that lead you into a flow state really easily because you have this focus. First of all, it's one of the places in this day and age where you can avoid notifications and pop-up interruptions, at least for now. I predict that is going to change pretty soon, but for now you can actually find yourself in a completely different environment that is totally immersive.

Aaron: We're now thinking about more ideas around taking that physical embodiment side even further. We haven't really talked publicly too much about this new area that we're investigating. Flow – this idea that you can get lost in something and time passes.

I'm interested right now in how we can get away from the computing paradigms that we've had for the last sixty years – hunched over a monitor and keyboard – into using your body in a computational context. Also, creating flow states that are very responsive.

Not to go into the dystopic social media side, but there's a hidden cost that we're not thinking about in society. Yes, we're thinking about data privacy. Yes, we're thinking about all kinds of social ramifications. But I think the interruption aspect is something that we're going to look back on. We'll think it's mind-blowing that we disrupted all of our flow states and all of our attention time with various forms of digital introduction that we didn't actually want and weren't that conscious of.

My public art making has slowed, as you may have noticed, since I started this company.

Building museum installations was gratifying, but you get a very small percentage of the population, at best, that can get access to that kind of visceral real-life experience.

With virtual reality, the promise was democratization of experience. You could actually have something that was related to your body and to the life scale, and the kind of impact and visceral sensation you get by going into a museum, but you can deliver that to millions of people across the planet instantly, and that felt like it was something worth experimenting with.

*

Aaron: The idea that you can feel embodied and present in a completely virtual environment is already here. It's not evenly distributed, but there are people who are experiencing that.

The other thing about virtual reality is it is a spectrum of immersion. Some might argue that video games are already a form of virtual reality. It's a field of view into that world. And then when you wrap it around yourself and get lost in it, there is some point where your embodiment is a different form of reality.

You're no longer using a controller to fire your bow and arrow. You're literally grabbing it, pulling it back and shooting it. And you can feel like you're there. If you want to get something off the table, you can walk up to the table, you can squeeze your hand like you're grabbing something and you can pick it up. You can eat it and you can throw it.

To me, it's about forgetting that you're not actually in this context. That's what immersion really is. So I think that's already happening.

We're not fully there yet in terms of tracking one's body, but it's a pretty compelling virtual recreation. And I think we will see that stuff get infinitely better over the next couple of years.

Damian: I can totally understand, in those immersive experiences, where you can get into the flow of that experience, but for the majority of the world, that is going to take them out of the flow of learning, studying, earning an income, talking, communicating with people.

Aaron: We're very wedded to more traditional ideas of existence. If you took the ten-year-old me, hanging out in the very early nineties, and you threw me into the same area of Los Angeles today, it's a completely different world. People are sitting there staring at their devices. They're zipping around on these electric scooters that they're paying for with these devices. There are screens everywhere. They can't get around without maps. They call Uber to come pick them up. The whole world has been transformed by these technologies that we're not really aware of, but we are living in a virtual world. We're not yet at the stage of real-time augmentation of that data, but we have these devices that we strap on our wrists and carry in our pockets and we hold them up to the world to tell us what we believe in.

I think, arguably, the kind of communication that I grew up with, to a large extent, was typing to people through keyboards. Now it's typing to people on a screen. And virtual reality is actually using your voice.

These technologies are actually starting to bend back towards [being] more human. Right now, it's a conversation between humans and machines, which is kind of bent. For a huge part of my generation we've bowed to the technology – I will learn how to program in this language, I will speak computer, and then I will use keyboards and interfaces that are made more for computers than they are for people.

Right now, it's all going towards voice. I think the virtual reality interface is going towards emotion, human hand motions. It's going towards more natural interfaces.

I would actually argue that, in some strange way, being in a rich virtual environment may be more naturally human than a lot of the computer world that we've spent a lot of our time in.

Damian: I've seen VR and technology also be really powerful tools for empathy, because you can see right there what's happening to someone and give live reactions. Where do you think that it's going? How does VR contribute to either the mob mentality of separation of people, or do you think it has the power to bring us together?

Aaron: Both. I mean, I think it's similar to film. We talk about empathy a lot because Chris [Milk] gave that TED Talk about virtual reality as an empathy machine.

Which was really borrowed from Roger Ebert, who was using that empathy machine for the movie camera. It holds true.

But I think that plays into this idea of mob mentality and empathy. These tools can be used for good or evil, to misguide or to educate. And I think the challenge is that they become just way more effective.

Damian: Is it possible for a computer to display any sort of empathy? There are companies that exist today where employees don't have a boss who is a person. Their boss is an AI. Uber is the biggest example of that. People are driving every day and have no interaction with a boss at any point, a human. Every decision that they take is made, and their future is determined by, an AI. There's no empathy whatsoever involved in that decision making. If you play on VR, the experience is quite insular. I can totally envision, again, how that experience would be phenomenal, but the empathy side is going to be predetermined by a machine, and predetermined by developers who – you excluded – are not generally always the most empathetic people.

Aaron: The empathy is in the human. That's definitely not in the machine, right? It's an interesting conversation and thought experiment to imagine an inorganic thing having empathy. It gets into a lot of questions about consciousness and value systems and, I guess, whether algorithms can exhibit empathy. It's really [how to] program attributes of the side effects of empathy into algorithms, but I'm not sure if that actually qualifies as real empathy.

Most of the experiences that we've been focused on have been either about showing stories of real people to people, to the virtual reality, or actually connecting real humans to each other in virtual spaces, which I think is really exciting and valuable.

If one does think that one of the root sources of happiness is providing value to a community, then people are at the root of that and the idea of separating out humans and human values is a pretty scary and dangerous thing, because it questions where happiness will come from, where true happiness will come from.

You look at Amazon, at all the food delivery services at home. I have wondered if people will even see other people in the future. Will there be classes of people that are just isolated in their ivory towers and get all of their things given to them and provided for them and only communicate with each other on rare occasions when they summon each other? Will there be completely different ways of life, or will we all be homogenizing?

Damian: Virtual reality is everywhere.

Aaron: It is, yeah. We're already living in it. The question is just, do we accept it? Do we embrace it consciously?

Damian: So, you don't have any kids, right?

Aaron: Not yet, no.

Damian: When your kids come to the age that you think it's acceptable for them to be on the internet – or connected, let's say – what advice do you think you'll give them?

Aaron: It'll be interesting. I imagine that that's going to be quite a while from now. So I can only imagine what the internet is going to be.

Damian: But you're helping to shape it, right? I mean, at least, my perception of what you guys are building is basically the sort of cable operator of VR. So somewhere between Netflix and HBO, or something, for VR. It hopefully won't be called VR, it'll be called something a little bit more accessible.

Aaron: We're still working on that.

Damian: You are at the forefront of this, sort of, race. And assuming that you believe in this future – and that's the future that you're creating for your potential kids – what would you tell them? What do you think it's going to look like?

Aaron: I think immersive technologies are going to be a while before they truly displace much of what we currently do. I think, eventually, one could imagine that the screens in our houses and in our pockets go away and that there is some kind of more wearable display that augments our world and gives us access to digital environments in a more intuitive, more impactful way.

So, that's, let's say, twenty years from now, I could imagine that kind of reality.

Damian: What should they look out for?

Aaron: There's the same stuff we grapple with today, but more extreme versions of it.

It's probably data.

It'll be interesting to see if the trends that we're on continue, with data aggregation. And does something completely unexpected and new emerge – probably out of blockchain technology – that allows us to own more of our own data? A lot of people are thinking about that.

Damian: So what sort of data, actually, are you tracking? I can imagine that in an immersive world of an amazing VR experience, where you're replicating something like my son's obsessive interaction with Fortnite, you're going to be able to check emotion and – if it's connected enough – increases in his blood pressure, and to actually build a complete character profile as to what sort of individual my son is. Is he stimulated more with fear, or does he shy away from fear? If he's stimulated more by that sensation, then you know that he's probably going to be more susceptible to X drug or Y toy.

And targeting them becomes so much more insane than it is today.

Do you track that sort of information?

Aaron: Currently, no. I think . . . as a company, to date, that's not been our goal. We don't even have advertising yet. I don't know that we ever will.

Damian: It will come.

Aaron: Not necessarily. I think . . . it's polarizing between advertising and subscription, and right now we are actually, very much more thinking about subscription.

I know there have been lots of conversations at various large tech companies, at a different place and time, about whether they should offer a premium service that's completely sans advertising for people who are willing to pay for it.

Which also paints this dystopian future, where only the poor are advertised to.

Damian: Or it paints a place where only quality advertising exists. I believe in the premise that everybody actually likes advertising but they hate bad advertising. If it's relevant . . .

Aaron: The fact that we're tailoring it to you, as in your best interest, to get a feel for the stuff you like. And it will provide value.

*

Damian: Do you think there's a limit to how much you can be in that experience?

Aaron: With VR, the question that you are asking is the one that many people were asking. It's a physiological question. I think the immediate answer would probably be a physiological one. Like, 'Oh I've spent enough time on the headset now.' It's gotten to the point where it's good enough, where it's not about the physiological question. It's about the content question.

I think that's actually good and important, because that medium can't exist if it's still at those baseline physiological questions. Like, 'Oh God, am I getting sick?' Or, 'Is this weighing on my head too hard?' Those problems, I think, are solved. To the extent that any computer device has solved that problem, like, probably staring at a screen for five hours a day is terrible for you as well – and certainly my posture reflects the hunched over-ness. One of the things I've been using VR for lately is trying to improve my posture.

So, there are actually a lot of physiological benefits that could come from prolonged VR use. I'm a little bit reluctant to talk too much publicly about this, because we're still doing some interesting research.

You talked earlier about how your son would drop any sport that he could do. I think you could have sport-like things that are digital that are really interesting and fun. Our bodies aren't going away yet. If you look at the trends, glamour now means fitness, it means eating well, it means treating your body as a temple. I try and have adequate posture by getting a standing desk. But there are ways to use technology that can actually respect our bodies more than we have in the past.

Damian: There's this idea that you are the product. In the VR world, is that not more the case?

Aaron: It could be. I think it's just another medium. It's a more immersive and more body-centric way of computing. But you can be the product, or you can not be.

Damian: You are certainly setting a standard in terms of quality. There are not many companies producing the quality of output that you are.

Aaron: I certainly hold us responsible for thinking about all these topics and hopefully making smart decisions. But, unfortunately, I think it will be up to the large tech companies that are making the hardware – and therefore the platform – to make the smart decisions. And ideally also enable the level of control. Just the idea that we all exist more and more in somebody else's sandbox. As entrepreneurs, you're not necessarily in a completely free and open marketplace. You're existing in one that is controlled by one of a small number of partners.

●●●

No one can tell us, in detail, what the future holds, but there are a few people who hold a vivid view of the past. Out of all the popular thinkers of our time, Stephen Fry is the person I want in charge of finding the soul of whatever comes next in tech, because he has spent his life investigating meaning. He ensures we don't discard all that is meaningful from our past as we plunge ahead.

For me, he has been a contextualizer. He provides intellectual context that feels vital, he makes ideas vital, and describes our place in this continuum. Not every business gets the opportunity to install someone like Fry on their board, or in their conference room, to dispense general wisdom. But any business operating in this new environment, any business that wants to understand why we need to remember the offline world as we plunge forward online, could do worse than turn to Fry. He's able to eloquently remind me how we've always been locked in a bitter duel with technological advancement, for hundreds of years, accepting what works and rejecting what doesn't.

Good business in the new trust environment means listening to those who can both assuage and challenge us on some of these ideas. Fry is a technophile but in our conversations I've always got the sense he's thought about his own barter. How much of himself was he willing to give up? How much of his own data would he allow the miners to mine? All of this should be taken with a grain of salt.

It's easy to be elusive, or to refrain from getting into the trenches of Twitter, when you're already broadcasting to 13 million people. Fry is in a privileged position. But he's also chosen to be aligned with what is healthiest, or brightest, in this new world.

What I like about him is the way he refuses to disconnect our current age from the past. We are not – even though much of Silicon Valley might like us to believe – living in some brand-new age, we are not brand-new creatures, we do not have new values.

The tools we are creating do not elevate us in any new and vaulted ways. We're ruled by the old gods, Fry reminds us. Nothing has changed; these are new tools for old urges. The urge to data mine, to know more than we should, has been in humans since we became human.

'You've mentioned you're writing about the relationship between what one might call the cold machine world and the human heart,' Stephen Fry said to me when we met. I agreed. I tried to explain, in the most eloquent and interesting way possible, what we were up to at WeTransfer: the no-sign-up, the refusal to collect data. I told him that, since 2009, straight through to the moment when Cambridge Analytica closed down, the tech industry was not in the slightest bit interested in talking to us. Then, suddenly, everybody became interested in companies that were online and not using data.

On Holding on to the Best of the Past
A Conversation with Stephen Fry

Stephen: So suddenly, a lack of vulgarity and commercial sort of violence, as it were, and the presence of empathy and sweetness of tone becomes a selling point.

Damian: It just happened.

Stephen: It just happened. And that's very pleasing.

Damian: I think one of the most critical actions for us all is to determine who's in charge.

Stephen: The buzzword at the moment is agency, isn't it?
    Whether we have agency in our online world and our online existence or whether we don't, whether we're puppets with invisible strings pulling us and moving us around that we're unaware of. It is very interesting.
    I come from the point of view that I think the human mind and body and all the bits in between that we give different names to – the spirit, the soul, the personality, character – are infinitely stronger than any technology we've yet arrived at.
    I often use the image of the fact we can stand in a field – we could go to one now, outside London, some-where in the countryside, where there are no roads and no phones – and look. And without any change in our

brain or thinking, but purely instinctively, if there was a breath of wind that turned a leaf over in the distance from being dark green to being the silvery underside, miles away, we'd see it. Because, you know, we've evolved either to look for lunch or to look out for being lunch for someone else.

So we're able to concentrate, focus, here, on the most extraordinary detail.

But half an hour later, on the train, we're on Oxford Street, there's a thousand people in our eyeline and music coming out of every shop, phone on, and traffic going. We're crossing and talking to someone. It's a miracle what our brain is doing and not doing.

People forget that a lot of brain processing is in the inhibition, not action – as in stopping you from falling over, stopping you from doing this, blanking that out, not seeing that, not taking account of this. And we don't even have to think about doing that. It's extraordinary how our brains respond. They haven't evolved for Oxford Street, and yet they cope with it, and it's quite remarkable.

The idea that we're being controlled by invisible forces in the internet may be worrying for us, but our ancestors always thought that anyway. That's what they thought the gods were. And they thought that was exactly what we were, that every time we moved, we were being watched and that everything we did was registered. There was providence in the fall of a sparrow. It says that in the Bible, doesn't it?

*

275

Damian: Do you use Facebook?

Stephen: No. I killed that recently.

Damian: Instagram? You left it?

Stephen: I use Instagram only because if I'm doing a project, the publicity department asks me to use it. I've only got 100 million followers, I think. You can look it up. I don't know. It's not very important to me, and I can't see what the point is.

Damian: You're still on Twitter?

Stephen: Yes. I do it a lot. I do it in a friendly way, and I've learned to be at peace with not following anybody, not following any threads, not looking at anybody's tweets. It's a notice. I put a notice up, and I run away. I don't watch people come up to it and look at it to make comments. You just put it up, and if people want to read it, they read it. Unlike noticeboards, they can't take it down. It's like one of those school noticeboards in the glass cases, locked.

When I first had an email address, which was in the 1980s, which is the world before there was a worldwide web or anything, I slowly watched it grow. I really thought it was Pandora, which is the Greek word for 'all-gifted'. She was this all-gifted woman who Zeus had created. He wanted to punish mankind, so he sent down this jar, which she wasn't allowed to open.

As the worldwide web arrived and Web 2.0 came on, and the first social media, I really thought that now, online, you have a city. There's museums, art galleries, concert halls, libraries, gathering places, red-light districts of course, no-go areas for children, like any good city. But it's all-gifted. There's everything there, and people can connect to each other with hobbies and interests and ideas that used to be in some badly smeared, printed fanzine that you had to wait a month to arrive as a quarterly thing. Now, you can connect with people all over the world with shared interests, and it will melt away differences. Mankind will become one, and we'll no longer hate each other.

And then, at some point, like Pandora's box – which is what we called this jar, whatever you call it – the lid got opened and, in the myth, out flew all the ills of the world. You know, lies, war, starvation. All the miseries of the world arrived, or were given to us, after Pandora's box. It was like that. Instead of it being this perfect thing, it turned out to be this ghastly thing, in one's worst moods. It turned out to be actually full of stinging, nattering, wheeling, chattering creatures that bit you. In Pandora's box, she closed the lid so firmly, she was so frightened by these animals.

Damian: Who's going to close the lid?

Stephen: She closed it too quickly, and she left inside hope, which beats its wings inside to this day, not being released. It's a very good image, because it's basically just saying that everything casts a shadow. Of course, the light of the internet was so bright at first, you didn't notice the shadows it was casting. Nobody did. Now we see nothing but the shadows. We forget the light.

*

Damian: Could it be self-regulated?

Stephen: That's the interesting point. How much could you sandbox your world? How much do you have to give up of your independent agency in order to gain some of the benefits, which will be astounding, of AI and related technologies? Granted, it's a really interesting point. When you talk about AI, you're also talking about some of the developments in the Internet of Things that are getting more and more remarkable because of the convergence of so many of these technologies.

A lot of the world will have the personal touch, and it will allow you to interface with the world wherever you are, and it all comes from a place that you can't really imagine.

*

Damian: Who can be trusted?

Stephen: Apple, for all that they get, obviously, a huge amount of hatred from all kinds of people in the weirdest way, they've chosen a path for their devices with privacy, which has denied them . . . They would be three times bigger as a company if they had decided to allow all kinds [of access], but in fact Tim, I know, is really strong on this. It doesn't matter how much the stockholders say, 'Think about how much we could get if we opened up just this much.' No. This is our contract with our users. Absolute privacy. They control everything. That's why the FBI were going, 'Fuck you. We need to open this phone,' and Apple was saying, 'No, fuck you. You can't.'

Damian: They are the good guys?

Stephen: I really do think they are. Of course, people are.

*

Stephen: Interestingly, I have a friend who's in security services, the secret service, from university. He's very quiet, honestly. Perhaps you have to be. I said to him, 'I'm asking you, because – of course, you know nothing about MI5 – but let's pretend you know someone in MI5.' He goes, 'All right.' I said, 'Would it be fair to say that people are rediscovering the tradecraft of the Le Carré days – one-time pads, dead letter boxes, those sorts of things – rather than relying on digital technology, which is hackable?' He said it would be very fair to say that. Very fair.

A couple of months later, he said, 'I've been thinking

about this a lot. It is absolutely true. A lot of agents in the field now don't use phones, don't use computers.' I thought, that's fantastic.

Damian: How do they communicate, then?

Stephen: By the old ways, the ways they used to. Old spycraft. Human intervention, writing down one-time pads, code books, memory, all those things that used to work in fieldcraft. You can't rely on, 'Here's a phone, it's totally secure.' Bollocks, it is. I thought it all really interesting. In the case that you want an agent in the field somewhere who's actually doing old-type spying, you're not going to give him GPS or Apple Watch. Exactly. Nothing like that stuff. Nothing hackable. It's much harder. You can't really hack a good, old-fashioned code in the one-time pad style. It's unhackable, and that's rather good. It is.

*

Damian: You must be able to focus.

Stephen: Actually, focus is a very interesting word. One of the things I like about myth is it comes from people sitting around the fire. That made me examine the whole nature of this. The very first god, born as opposed to Titan, was not Zeus, it was the lesser-known Hestia, or Vesta. She was the goddess of the hearth, and it's minor compared to Poseidon being [god of] the sea. To our ancestors, the hearth is the absolute – literally central. Ancient language reveals this. Hearth is cognate, as a linguist would say, with heart. It's the same word – heart, hearth – as it is in Greek. The Greek word for hearth is 'cardia', as in cardiac and cardiology, heart.

The Latin word for hearth is 'focus'. We've taken that as a metaphor.

We've taken the Latin word for hearth to be a metaphor for anything that we concentrate our energies around. We call that a focus, a hearth.

It's only in the last twenty, thirty, forty years that we've stopped having hearths. Even the television used to be a hearth. It literally was the nation's fireplace. In one room, the same people gathered around the fire, the flicker that came from the television, and we all saw the same pro-gramme at the same time. It was a national conversation, a national hearth. That no longer exists.

The dining-room table no longer exists. Families go into their house; everyone has their own bedroom, their own game console, their own laptop, and they don't see each other.

I think that – more than any other aspect of the digital world – may well be deleterious to our species. The fact that we no longer, every day, sit around with family, friends, whatever, and in common share stories, share the day, plan the future.

You can plan. You can talk. You can bond. You can define your separateness and your commonality.

That's all been broken up. Rather, we talk about

corporate powers, but we no longer have that glue, which
is so important.

*

Stephen: I believe in the human spirit. I believe in the
human mind. But I don't believe in it in a wishy-washy
way. I do think . . . what I would say is this.

If we're talking about the poetry of the world, or anything like that, poetry is as hard won as gold. It's a real
thing, gold, but to get it, you have to have knowledge of a
geologist as to where it's most likely to be. Then you have
to excavate. Someone has to bark their knuckles and
make their fingers bleed and live in hot, hideous conditions to bring out the mineral, which then has to be
smelted. It's incredibly hard work. But then you have gold.
It's not handed down by an angel, ever, ever.

Same with poetry and truth – poetic truth and scientific
truth. They're real. They're achievable. But only through
the sweat of your brow can you experience knowledge,
understanding, trial and error, failure. You come up with a
real poetic insight, a real moment of breathtaking clarity,
into who we are and how we can be better. It connects us
and makes us smile, but it's not easily done.

It's the same with scientific truth. Endless hard work,
endless failure. The only problem with culture, and the
speed and everything else, is we somehow think that
along with it will come a short cut. This is the problem
with the literature of mindfulness and empathy, the literature of 'Things They Didn't Teach You At Harvard' that

will make you a great CEO. All bullshit, trying to suggest these are short cuts: when you do this, this can happen quicker. The real secret is, it can't happen quicker, but that doesn't make it bad.

There is the destination, and here you are. It's not going to be a straight journey. It's not going to be a straight line. You'll have to find out how to get there. There will be a lot of effort. You will get there.

Damian: Is part of the problem we face the fact that the power in the tech industry is in the hands of those who are too young?

Stephen: In a way, yes. I think that, unfortunately, by being incredibly spoiled in their early twenties and their late twenties, they've become billionaires. At some point, without them really knowing how it happened, they've become entitled, and they think their view of the world and politics and society must be correct because they're a genius, because they've achieved something through their own brilliance, and they must be right.

If you look at Steve Jobs' commencement speech, when he talks about the horror when he was sacked from the company he founded. How hurt he was, how angry he was, and how he now thinks it was the best thing to ever happen to him. His wilderness.

You know, not that he's a faultless human, I'm not suggesting that. But he's an example of someone who didn't quite do the Zuckerberg thing and have just a completely perfect, smooth transition at all. He had to fight, and he had to focus and rethink and reset, recalibrate.

Damian: Do you think that could be because Steve Jobs was more of a designer than a technologist?

Stephen: Design, absolutely. Not design merely in the sense of how it looks. Design in the sense of how it works for you.

Damian: I'm not saying that this is always the case, but I can see that in companies that are being run by developers who are trained to code and to build algorithms, that most of them are not the most empathetic on earth.

Stephen: No. It's very rare that nature gives the brain the ability to code, which is an astonishing gift of mathematics and abstract thought, giving abstract ideas a numerical value that has a function. To give someone that gift and give them a social gift and an insight into the human spirit, or even a curiosity about human history and human culture and philosophy, is very rare. Very few of them have it. They're just not curious about it. I just think that's where everything lives, and they don't look up. There's a film infinitely better than *The Revenant* that never got a single award, years ago, called *Jeremiah Johnson*. Robert Redford plays a guy who goes out into the wild exactly like the Leo character. There's an old boy he meets, covered in skins and pelts and fur and things, in this terribly cold place, this very frightening wilderness. He has this line: 'Keep your nose to the wind and your eye to the skyline.' Don't look down.

Steve Jobs kept his nose to the wind and his eye to the skyline, but at the same time, he was very, very focused. It's that weird thing: how can you be both? He kept his nose to the wind and his eye to the skyline. Steve Wozniak was the one who was doing all the tech, building the circuit in the seventies.

I've never met anybody who's successfully prophesied anything technologically. I remember, in November 1999, sitting in the BBC Radio 4 studio with someone from Adobe – I can't remember her name, she was the head of Adobe UK at the time, which was a big thing to be – Douglas Adams and myself, and we were being asked about the twenty-first century. Douglas said, 'I think we ought to say straight away that you're asking people interested in computers about the twenty-first century. We should bear in mind that the fact that the year 1999 is followed by the year 2000 has caught a lot of us horribly by surprise. Our ability to forecast the future really must be in question if we didn't see 2000 coming as a number.'

Every year, there's someone writing about what we're going to see, and I just have no idea, but the one stable thing is the human spirit and the human heart, human ambition, human greed, human appetite, human propensity to be addicted to pleasure and repelled by pain and labour and toil and all the difficult things.

All of that is stable, has never changed, as far as I can tell by reading the first poetry ever written, which is Homer, all the way to the modern age through history. All the evidence we have about ourselves as a species is we have never altered.

We haven't changed.

Our technology has never changed us. The industrial revolution didn't change the human spirit. It enslaved people in different ways. That enslavement was of an order that was predictable, according to: if you treat a human like that, they will behave like that. It was a new way and a new scale, perhaps. But it didn't alter us. It didn't alter the fact that we murder. We murder for gain and for sexual pleasure – whatever – anger, greed. All those things are the same. The same gods . . . Dionysus. The god of addiction and frenzy.

•••

18: We, the People

After listening to these voices, I realized I needed to examine what was possible in my own life. I kept returning to the idea of what we're able to achieve collectively.

We have the power

The first step we need to take is acknowledging that we are in control.

Imagine, for a moment, the worst ever retail experience. Start with some appalling customer service. Your loyalty card gets lost, your name is absent from the directory for a discount, your store card is charged twice, the changing-room curtain keeps falling down and you're left exposed. If this were to happen as frequently as it does in a company like Facebook, the likelihood is you'd boycott the store. You'd simply find another.

Now, you might argue, there is no other Facebook. There is just one Instagram. All my friends and birthdays are linked to Facebook. I can't possibly leave.

You can. Increasingly this is being posed as a moral issue. What about our duty to others? 'The possibility of a duty to leave Facebook arises once one recognizes that Facebook has played a significant role in undermining democratic values around the world,' philosopher S. Matthew Liao wrote in November 2018, in the *New York Times*. 'Facebook has been used to spread white supremacist propaganda and anti-Semitic messages in and outside the United States. The United Nations has blamed Facebook for the dissemination of hate speech against Rohingya Muslims in Myanmar that resulted in their ethnic cleansing.'

It goes on. Just a reminder: Ben & Jerry's haven't yet been found to be persecuting Rohingyas.

It's as if the shop that offered terrible customer service is now beating up passers-by on the sidewalk as well.

Liao also makes reference to the collective 'us'. In his mind, using Facebook is a collective action that destroys trust. It's like if a bunch of us were to stop paying income tax. A few people? No problem. But millions?

'A few people failing to pay taxes might not make much of a difference to a government's budget,' writes Liao. 'But such an action may nevertheless be wrong because it is a failure to participate in a collective action that achieves a certain good end. In a similar vein, choosing to remain on Facebook might not directly undermine democratic values. But such an action could also be wrong because we might be failing to participate in a collective action (that is, leaving Facebook) that would prevent the deterioration of democracy.'

Smart companies will embrace this chance to redefine trust.

I believe it will benefit businesses to ease this process and help the 'us' rediscover its 'us'-ness. A gap is opening up. If consumers take control, smart businesses will be right there.

Case in point: is giving up Facebook impossible? Or are there already companies there to aid you in the transition?

You can copy all of your contacts out of Facebook, add your birthdays to a calendar, use Diaspora instead of Instagram, EyeEm or Vero. Of course they won't be as easy to use. Of course not as many people use them. Someone has to make the first move.

I took the leap. I made an active choice to leave Instagram and Facebook because I believed it was better for my mental health and as an example to my kids. What this means is that I do miss out on a lot of what's happening. People still update around me via Instagram and Facebook. Friends still invite people to parties via Facebook and share holidays and photos via Instagram. I just have to go back to staying in contact the old-fashioned way. I call more, message and email constantly, like I did in the pre-Facebook days. Sure, I miss out on a few things. But in the long run, my friends remain my friends and I remain sane. I know this sounds like a chore, like giving up something essential, but there are hungry companies ready to take the best of, say, Facebook, and leave the worst behind.

What I would love to see happening in the next few years is society using social media to fix itself and demand change through action online. We pay for it. Let's have it our way.

As we begin to redefine trust for ourselves, we might have time to survey the landscape and notice if there's anyone out there who will step up to be the Jane Jacobs of our time – Jane being a writer and activist who arguably changed the face of the modern city. We need individuals to demand respect for these neighbourhoods we've created. Or perhaps we'll find a collective variation on the idea of Citizen Jane.

There's a chance a few of these figures already exist amongst us. In a book where I've been able to make a list of my own important interviewees, here's one more, perhaps one of the most important. Baroness Martha Lane-Fox is, to me, an example of a digital Citizen Jane. For those who don't know her, she and Brent Hoberman founded Lastminute.com in 1998. She sold the business in 2003, bought a karaoke club and began a crusade for a better internet.

Back in 2013, we spent a lot of time admiring Martha's work from a distance as she took on the monumental job of redeveloping and redesigning the UK government's digital presence. Martha and her team were given a remit to encourage as many people as possible to go online, and improve the convenience and efficiency of public services by driving online delivery. What did this mean? It meant that she created gov.uk.

Wow. I know that's what you're thinking. So what?

So, you have to imagine yourself in a post office or in an embassy. The building is dilapidated. There are ropes snaking across the floor for miles to guide the most miserable-looking people in existence towards four booths. It's staffed by the living dead. En route to the booths are pigeon holes filled with countless forms in every colour of the rainbow, booklets, brochures, useless posters telling you what to do – and not a pen in sight to help you in any way. Each booth is an island and the wrong answer will send you back to 'start'. This is what government looked and smelled like in the noughties. And the government's websites were worse: impossible to navigate, uncoordinated, illogical.

Martha and her teams reimagined, redesigned and rebuilt the entire system and housed it under one roof: gov.uk.

Still, to this day, it is used as a guide for the world as to how useful government can be and how important it is to help citizens and to put user experience first, rather than bureaucracy.

We talked for quite some time, but Martha is someone who cuts to the chase and to summarize her thinking I can hone in on two simple paragraphs.

'I think that there's a lot that we can do if we take a systems change approach, which is helping individuals feel more empowered. Governments and corporates can play a much bigger role, if you imagine the public health campaigns [of the past]. 'No smoking' campaigns. We need the equivalents; taking back control and helping people to understand the web better, be more aware of the transactions that are occurring around us.

There's a whole bunch of stuff companies can do to make more impact. Look at Marks & Spencer. Only 10 per cent of actual products are fair trade. Yet the fair trade effort has put the squeeze on the rest of the industry and today it's totally unacceptable to have a child labourer attached to the supply chain. We need to do the same in technology. Put the pressure on all those different angles, and the companies will step up and step in. And the good news . . . is that we are just talking about Google, Facebook, Amazon and, to a lesser degree, Netflix and Twitter.'

Putting pressure on Big Tech and government is exactly what Martha has been doing through Doteveryone, which brings me to the next step.

Don't fear the regulation

This word 'regulation' can make people turn green and feel their stomachs clench. I've seen interviews and conversations change very swiftly when I mention that the internet needs parameters and needs regulation.

But regulation can be just as flexible as innovation.

We must begin to redefine and reimagine the word in this new trust environment. I believe it's possible to strip 'regulation' of some of its more frightening connotations, and celebrate what it has done for us in the past.

When I think of regulation, I think of a conversation I had with Robbie Stamp, Chief Executive of Bioss International and a great friend of one of my heroes, the author Douglas Adams. Adams died in 2001 but Stamp is still around to hold the torch and amplify his ideas. Stamp served as executive producer on the latest movie version of *The Hitchhiker's Guide to the Galaxy.*

What does a cult classic have to do with life in our new trust environment? Sometimes, in order to move forward, you have to consult those who were doing interesting things in the past.

Robbie remembered back to the late nineties, when he and Douglas Adams were already assessing the state of data, responsible tech and a possible precursor to the GDPR equivalent. What on earth happened? What got in the way?

With Adams, Stamp gathered together a group of interested thinkers in a company that was originally called the Digital Village.

'We were thinking really, really early, about this issue of the enormous capacity the internet was clearly going to have to gather data about you,' he told me when I caught up with him and the talk strayed towards forms of regulation.

For Stamp – very crudely put – there are two kinds of data. 'There's the data I volunteer,' he told me. 'I will tell you that I'm a certain age. I will say I'm married. I'm interested. I volunteer it, in some kind of quid pro quo relationship, which I understand. And I feel that in return for volunteering it, I will get something in return. And then, there's everything that you infer. And I think it's really those inference patterns, as much as anything else, that have run out of control, and it's the pace and the speed I worry about.'

For Stamp, the gatekeepers of this data grew too big, too fast. Adams was similarly sceptical. These new gatekeepers didn't need to fully examine the role of trust. The chair of, say, a massive bank understands she's dealing with regulatory, social, political, environmental and technological change in different constituencies. A person in this position will make judgements that will not play out immediately.

'You won't be able to say that was a good judgement or a bad judgement or a good shot or a bad shot, sometimes for decades.' For Stamp, there are people out there in all sorts of industries who are dealing with huge amounts of uncertainty

293

and ambiguity and nuance and change. They have responsibility and take it very seriously.

Today, we've given our trust to people who have moved too quickly to come to terms with how they should act. In some cases we've become enamoured of their untrustworthy behaviour. We've celebrated breaking things so much that we're now surveying the broken landscape with a newfound suspicion. Wow, we think, look at all those broken things.

The speed at which Facebook went from being nothing to something didn't allow for an examination of trust.

'Even from the word go,' says Stamp, 'he [Zuckerberg] knew he was gathering valuable data. But what Facebook was, was incredibly slow, and you can see it even up till the Trump election, when they were still playing the "We're just a platform. There's nothing to see. Move along. Move along." '

Stamp doesn't describe Facebook's activities as anything so genteel as strip mining. For him, it's worse. 'The board at Facebook got stuck in a business model which was about farming humans for their data. So, in the same way that farmers are conditioning farmed sheep for their wool and cows for their milk, we were farmed for our data, in return for the fodder. You know, we got our fodder, and our fodder was Facebook. It was our hay. It was our grass. It was our basket.'

Tech companies, for Stamp, just aren't sophisticated enough to take on the responsibilities of trust. They might be good at optimizing, but in the new trust landscape they can't handle the complexity. He went back to his example of the chair of a bank. 'He knows that he is entering a geopolitical environment for which he has certain responsibilities and in which he plays a huge role. He is not running a financial platform. He is running a financial company. He is paid well and works hard. But the buck stops with him and not at the customer and the ATM.'

He went on: 'And then we have Zuckerberg, after a fourteen-year period of time, suddenly being accused of helping to undermine Western liberal democracy and being part of geopolitical shifts in Russia and America and China, vying for positioning as the tectonic plates around geopolitics and geography shift.'

Russia follows a deliberate policy of destabilizing. Facebook, as we've seen now, has been a very useful, trust-busting tool. 'And suddenly,' Stamp said, 'Facebook is caught up in a level of geopolitics which Zuckerberg, frankly, was doing everything he could to fend off and deflect and could not handle. He is simply not a knowledgeable, experienced enough CEO. His interests are not aligned with those of the people. And in my view there is no question that he is one of the most powerful men on earth in an industry less regulated than oil, tobacco, finance and pharma.'

We need to regulate to protect ourselves from the naive Zuck.

Stamp's words struck a chord and reminded me of a line from an episode of the podcast *Pivot* with Scott Galloway and Kara Swisher. Galloway said of the team at Facebook: 'These guys make tobacco executives look like Mr Rogers.'

It's not all about Zuckerberg. But at this point he's transformed himself into a walking cautionary tale – a figure who could, in the end, be even more hapless, villainous and hubristic than he was in the final scene of the Hollywood blockbuster based on his life.

But it's really not all about Mark Zuckerberg. It's about money, greed and opportunity. Without regulation, things have a tendency to go some kind of wrong.

Any fast-growing industry throughout the history of the earth has proven this.

I'm fully in line with this concept of regulation taken from Doteveryone.

Responsible Technology promotes a fair, inclusive and thriving democratic society.

It works in the best interests of the individual and of the public as a whole, safeguards against harm and is founded on fair and transparent value exchange between people and technology.

Being responsible, being regulated, does not mean that we throttle and limit possibilities. It means, simply, that fewer people get fucked over. It means that there is greater transparency, a better division of wealth and knowledge.

The investment community has to step up

Business leaders, VCs, bankers, investors, angels need to be far more responsible and look for good gains at small cost.

'We face enormous challenges over the next decade – most of all from the climate crisis,' Martha Lane-Fox told me. 'If we don't put responsibility at the heart of the design of technology, how will we solve these challenges? We must proceed with intent and a real focus on the consequences of what we are creating.'

Companies need to cease looking to please VCs and the stock market in the short term and look far, far further ahead. They need to trust in the future. Not only are far fewer companies able to invest in R&D in the way they used to (back in the 1970s, IBM would spend upwards of 25 per cent of profits on R&D), but because of the short-term thinking that's taking place, companies are not able to place long-term bets or make long-term commitments to really force change.

We need to be able to trust that companies will start to see the long view.

How can a tech company, 80 per cent supported by VCs with a maximum ten-year – more probably a five-year – horizon seriously make a difference? How can they get behind fixing issues such as homelessness in a city like San Francisco, which will take decades, unless the CEOs, VCs and investment community take a longer term view? And importantly, how can we emphasize that they are part of the problem and can be part of the solution too?

So how are we going to step up? How are we going to do good?

We are asked this question frequently. 'It's easy for WeTransfer to give away media to support issues, because you can't sell it all. I'm in e-finance. What can I do?'

There are two ways of operating.

Fill your pockets as much as you can

Look after yourself, build a business that is self-sufficient, isolated, profitable (at all costs) and then later, purely for the purposes of taxation, establish a charity, a foundation and a way for you to be able to pay less tax. Oh and, of course, do amazing amounts of good, because that's what really motivates you.

A perfect example of this is Jean Paul Getty or Walmart or even Warren Buffett. All proudly frugal, hard business people – buying low and selling high – who all, at a certain moment in their lives (generally late), were coerced either for tax reasons or to avoid the PR mess of being some of the richest people on earth and not helping anyone, into deciding to give something back.

Then there is the alternative.

Cultivate constant giving

When I was a teenager, I stumbled across George Soros. Okay, I know he's held up as the bogeyman by every conspiracy theorist and alt-right troll at the moment. But let's take a deep breath and reconsider the guy. When I first became aware of him, it was because he appeared back in 1992 on the front page of nearly every newspaper as 'the man who broke the Bank of England'. I had no real idea what this meant.

At the time I was studying Business Studies and reading the *Financial Times* at school. (We had a particularly detail-orientated teacher who gave us many a lesson on how to fold the *FT* and read it on a busy train.) I read George's biography *Soros on Soros*, back in 1995, and loved how George from the very first day he started making money donated and gave back, to support his beliefs and roots. George Soros launched his philanthropic work in South Africa, in 1979. Since then he has given over $32 billion to fund the Open Society Foundations, which work in over 100 countries around the world.

I was once advised by a business partner that you shouldn't bother with philanthropy until you'd helped yourself. This was explained in the same vein as 'you need to learn to love yourself first before you can love others'. At the time, I felt physically ill, as I'd been raised to believe that, no matter what happened to us, we were privileged, far more fortunate than the majority of the world. In the words of novelist Isabel Allende: 'What is the point of having experience, knowledge or talent, if you don't give it away? Of having stories, if you don't tell them to others? Of having wealth, if you don't share it? I don't intend to be cremated with any of it.'

We have to do it as we go. You don't have to agree with Soros's politics, but his modus operandi is worth emulating. The old model of waiting till it's all said and done was fine for a previous age, but these are different times.

What I envision is a flow between companies and the

people who use them, a way of showing – almost constantly – that people's trust and belief are having an effect. We are not a company that is promising to do something in the future but, rather, endorsing and supporting it right now – and doing so in a way that is integral to the company, not an offshoot.

This kind of constant giving is not only a sign of generosity but a sign of a more responsive company, one that works alongside people.

I've got examples of causes, individuals and organizations that matter: Richard Curtis's Project Everyone; The Turtle Conservancy (because everyone loves turtles). And the big issues: digital sustainability, climate change and diversity.

This is a step towards stepping up. These days, businesses can't promise to be more trustworthy, better citizens, more engaged – in the future. It's got to be in their existing DNA. It's got to happen now.

Which brings me to the big one.

Viewing the internet as the real world

So long as we continue to view the internet as another dimension, or an alternative space, it will never improve. My children spend upwards of twenty hours per week connected; it's likely they spend more time playing online than playing outside.

There is an opinion amongst many of us, parents or not,

that the way to fix the issue of the internet is to wall ourselves in. Or live in a gated community.

Buy a cable connection that allows you to put filters on what your kids watch, when and for how long. Adjust your browser settings to prevent them looking at the wrong things. Set your parental settings and family sharing settings so that you can see everything.

Finally, in your fully connected home, install cameras to allow you to see what is happening at all times.

Is this really the new trust environment? Or the same as just moving into a gated, protected enclave. It won't change anything.

We need to be actively involved in the internet, active in the entirety of this boomtown, in all its parts: in the alleyways, underpasses, street corners and shopping malls. We need to be far more in charge and in control of what is happening.

I believe there needs to be some meeting place to consider and debate governance and regulation in order for us to be able to live safely together.

Something that is abundantly clear from all the conversations I've had is that no one wants the web to go away. That's not an option. The internet has become a second home to everyone. For the majority of us, our lives and our livelihoods are dependent upon it.

We need to forget the notion that the internet – this real place – needs to be free for everyone. Because just like 'trust', the word 'free' has been repurposed and redefined while we've been looking elsewhere. 'Internet free' is not free. Free-mium is not a thing. Free is ad-funded and data-driven. That free lunch we all heard about in first year economics classes? Yep. It's still not free.

Any educated internetter today should have a thorough understanding of how things are funded online, yet recent studies, according to Doteveryone, have shown that up to 40 per cent of people who live their lives online have no idea how some websites make their money.

We need an honest appraisal of this place, which should go hand in hand with a little more digital self-worth. Privacy and data are more valuable than people think. They are what run this boomtown.

Users are starting to grasp this fact. But how can we exped-ite the process?

If we need to know more about the value of something that seems ubiquitous in our lives, education helps, as does trans-parency. Schools will need to educate, as will governments.

We need the equivalent of a big, effective 'Smoking Kills' sticker to knock this particular version of the Marlboro man off his horse.

Most importantly, let's quit it with the trite phrase: 'We are the product.'

This was a term coined long before the internet came along. In the 1973 short film *Television Delivers People*, sculptor Richard Serra and his collaborator Carlota Fay Schoolman were already referring to us, the consumer, and mass media as the product fuelling television.

You are the product of t.v.

*

Media asserts an influence over an entire cultural spectrum, without effort or qualification.

*

Corporate control advocates materialistic propaganda.

*

CORPORATIONS ARE NOT RESPONSIBLE TO GOVERNMENT.

CORPORATIONS ARE NOT RESPONSIBLE TO THEIR EMPLOYEES.

*

You are consumed.

You are the product of television.

Television delivers people.

He had a point, especially since customers were paying $40 to receive television, with limited choice. But come on: this is nearly fifty years ago. We cannot today still feel trapped and restricted, with limited choice.

Our data, intellectual property and imagery are fuelling these new companies. But just to be clear: you are not a finite product. You are expected to be a never-ending process. That implies passivity from here on in. And guess what? You don't have to be passive.

You are paying for free services with your time. And to be frank, you're worth a whole lot more.

Conclusion

The internet has made our lives ridiculously easier. The internet has created great wealth, great knowledge, has created new economies. Heck, the internet has even created new currencies. But like any awesome resource, it must be maintained, it must be cultivated. The concept of the internet being free and accessible to everyone is delightful, but we now know what 'free and accessible' means.

'I wouldn't say the internet has failed with a capital F, but it has failed to deliver the positive, constructive society many of us had hoped for.' This was Tim Berners-Lee, interviewed in *The Economist* back in June, 2018. If Berners-Lee is feeling down, is there any hope for the rest of us?

So what are we saying?

The companies that moved fast and grabbed huge swathes of this online world have now, as of 2019, demonstrated that they cannot be trusted. They have failed to bring even the most basic offline set of values into the online sphere. Some kind of new protection, new regulation, is needed to rebuild this place we love.

For this to take shape, it's essential to provide space for professionals working across different sectors to all inter-mingle and work collaboratively, to explore challenges and solutions in technology. Something that we need to encour-age is a greater sense of cross-pollination between industry, and a broader view of the impact of technology, if we are to develop and create a more responsible future for technology.

To quote Mary Meeker: 'It's crucial to manage for unin-tended consequences. But it's irresponsible to stop innovation and progress.'

Regulation doesn't have to look like the twentieth century, but let's remember – with honesty – the good bits of regula-tion and antitrust legislation. Let's not forget the pleasure that comes from smashing a monopoly or two.

Regulation should come in the form of a loop. But an open loop, as opposed to the current tech-led closed loops or inner circles or moats, as they are referred to.

We, the people, need to engage with the tech industry, and the tech industry needs to engage with government. This has to happen in a frequent, collaborative manner on every con-tinent of the world. And if it's working, the mutually sustaining process will yield great things.

There will need to be finances in place to sustain this process. And it will have to be sustained, as technology will continue to evolve and the complexities of the issues – social, mental, local, global, physical, human or cyborg – will not dissipate.

Transparency has been demanded of us. In this triangular structure, we're going to demand more transparency of the tech world.

It's going to be tough but it's up to us. Most of us are addicts, most of us are a teensy bit hypocritical, railing against Facebook, Apple, Amazon and Google while using their services every minute of every day. Most of us are overworked, overtired, uncertain of how to create something, unable to band together. Most of us don't know how to support our governments or bring about change. Most Americans don't know things are a little bit different in Europe. But small steps are being taken. New ways of dealing with privacy, new tactics to protect ourselves, are emerging. And help, in some cases, is on the way.

The companies who are beginning to help in this new trust landscape will be rewarded. There's money to be made. The future looks bright for companies who are forgoing rapacious data mining in return for authentic communication with their consumers. But they must exist and be given a chance to flourish in a system that is not tilted towards the big players. In a centralized system, these companies will get eaten up.

We've got our work set out for us.

Let's build a more trusting world.

Acknowledgements

As always in life, I often bite off more than I can chew. I learn to swim by jumping in. This book is no exception. It would not exist were it not for my exceptionally tolerant wife, partner and friend, Esther, who has always supported me and accompanied me across the globe. She's allowed me to pursue my work. Esther, thank you for always being there and for joining me on this adventure.

I could not have done this without my kids, Fabian and Sophia. You've shown me what's important in life, kept me focused on the present and the future, not the past. You've helped me to understand the impact technology can have on children. Hopefully, someday you'll understand why you weren't allowed on Instagram!

And I would not be who I am or where I am today without you, Mum and Dad. You have always done your best to put the ambitions for me, Nadia and Julian at the forefront and encouraged us to follow our dreams. I know you're still mad at me for writing that piece about boarding schools on Medium, but, hopefully, this acknowledgement will make up for it. :)

ACKNOWLEDGEMENTS

To Craig Taylor who is possibly one of the most patient, thoughtful and considerate human beings I have ever met. [HA, HA.] Throughout this book, Craig has pushed the limits of what I thought was possible and helped me to take my thinking to a deeper level. Truth be told this book would not exist if it weren't for Craig. Craig lives in a wooden hut on a remote island in Canada. Please buy his books so that he can move to the mainland one day.

And, lastly, to the many who have played decisive roles in this decade-long quest to make internet history. To Nalden, my business partner, I hope we'll continue to work together, like the Gilbert and George of tech; to Bas, for thinking up WeTransfer; to the original team of Dave, Anne, Rinke (RIP) and Stefan; to the friends I have made on the way, including Nelly, Gilles, Troy, Giles, Gail; and to all the individuals I have had the opportunity to lead and be led by. Thank you for serving as the inspiration and providing the foundation for *The Trust Manifesto*.

Index

311

PENGUIN PARTNERSHIPS

Penguin Partnerships is the Creative Sales and Promotions team at Penguin Random House. We have a long history of working with clients on a wide variety of briefs, specializing in brand promotions, bespoke publishing and retail exclusives, plus corporate, entertainment and media partnerships.

We can respond quickly to briefs and specialize in repurposing books and content for sales promotions, for use as incentives and retail exclusives as well as creating content for new books in collaboration with our partners as part of branded book relationships.

Equally if you'd simply like to buy a bulk quantity of one of our existing books at a special discount, we can help with that too. Our books can make excellent corporate or employee gifts.

Special editions, including personalized covers, excerpts of existing books or books with corporate logos can be created in large quantities for special needs.

We can work within your budget to deliver whatever you want, however you want it.

For more information, please contact
salesenquiries@penguinrandomhouse.co.uk